FREE MEN

Meditations on the Bible Today

FREE MEN

Meditations on the Bible Today

SUZANNE DE DIÉTRICH

Translated
with an Introduction by
OLIVE WYON

SCM BOOK CLUB
NAPERVILLE, ILL.

FIRST PUBLISHED 1961
© SCM PRESS LTD 1961

PRINTED IN GREAT BRITAIN BY
BILLING AND SONS LTD
GUILDFORD AND LONDON

CONTENTS

Part Three

THE LIBERTY OF THE CHRISTIAN

Part Four

Introduction

ON STUDYING THE BIBLE

by Olive Wyon

HERE IS A PASSAGE from a sermon by a celebrated preacher: 'Which of us goes home to occupy himself in a Christian manner after church? Who takes the pains to read the books, and applies himself to discover the sense of Holy Scripture? No one will dare to say he does his best. We find rich furniture in the houses of church-people, but we find nowhere good books, or at least among few; and those who have such books are as if they had them not, keeping them always shut up . . . Which of you who hears me now would be able to say by heart a Psalm or some other part of Scripture if I were to ask this of him?'

These words have a very modern ring. Yet they come to us from the fourth century, from the lips of the great preacher, St John Chrysostom. He was a very able preacher and people flocked to hear him; his sermons were noted for their simple, clear exposition of the Scriptures. We are all aware of the wide-spread ignorance of the Bible today, and we greatly need such clear guidance in Bible Study. Here, in this small book, there is a method of Bible Study, and guidance along some main lines, which is fresh and living, and up-to-date. If this book is simply *read* through quickly, it will fail of its purpose, for it is intended to be *studied, and above all, to lead its readers to study all the passages cited for themselves.* In another book by the same author, *Discovering the Bible,*[1] she has defined the aim of Bible Study very clearly: 'We study the Bible in order to

[1] *Discovering the Bible*, Suzanne de Diétrich.

7

listen to what God has to say to us, and to accept his claim on our lives.' In order to do this properly, however, she points out that 'we have to hear the whole story', and this means that 'we have to take the Old Testament seriously too'. For 'the Bible comes to us with such a tremendous claim . . . that if what it says is true, then indeed Jesus Christ is the centre not only of the Bible but of the whole history of mankind, the one God-given answer to our whole human quest—the Word made flesh'. And she quotes Dr Visser 't Hooft, who says: 'We find increasingly that every time we try to separate Jesus from the Bible-as-a-whole, we are really trying to get away from him. Thus we are committed to the Bible because we are committed to Jesus'.[1]

This particular book is an example of the work of Mlle Suzanne de Diétrich, who has taught so many how to study the Bible—both in her own French Protestant circles and in the wider circles of the World's Student Christian Federation and those who studied at the Ecumenical Institute at Bossey, during the first years of its life. She follows one particular line of approach to Bible Study, that is, *the topical approach*: 'the study outline selects its biblical material from various parts of the Bible around one central theme'. Here she is dealing with the meaning of *Freedom*, in the deepest sense of the word. However anxious we may be to relate this study directly to human problems, she warns us against making the Bible merely a springboard for discussion and the airing of our own views: 'a real knowledge of the Biblical message and its implications is therefore a pre-condition for this kind of study'.

This book may be used in two ways: for group study, or for private meditation. Ideally the group method should lead on to the more personal kind, but both may be carried on at the same time by the members of a group, and both kinds of study will be enriched. In other words, the Bible is a unity; hence we need to remind ourselves continually that 'the Bible is *its own interpreter*. Every part should be seen

[1] *None Other Gods* by W. A. Visser 't Hooft, pp. 68-69.

in the light of the whole. In reading a given book we should ask ourselves what specific truth about God, man, or the history of the people of God, this book is meant to convey'.[1] The whole problem of historical criticism is put in its right perspective in the words of a great Biblical scholar of the present day: 'It is idle to suppose that an objective criticism can pronounce for us judgments of ultimate truth. It cannot so present the message of the Bible that it compels our assent by logical proof. At best it can help to make us share the experience which the Bible represents. For the history of the people of God is recapitulated in the history of the soul. We know their trials, temptations, doubts and sufferings; like them we seek the promised land, go astray after other gods, and enter the dark night of exile. To us as to them the divine judgments and promises are spoken and the Saviour comes. The crisis of history becomes the crisis of our own souls. In it the Word of God sounds for us, but the answer is for us to give.'[2]

In group study[3] there should always be first of all a very careful study of the actual *Bible text*, in order to be quite sure of its meaning (here the leader or some other member of the group may bring help from various commentaries or from other versions). Then the subject should be placed in its actual historical setting (if there is one), and related to the message of the Bible as a whole. 'Only when this is done', he insists, 'should we ask ourselves what God means to say *to us, today*', through these passages or sayings.

A study group should meet regularly, if possible weekly. It should be small: not more than twelve, though between five and nine is perhaps the best—speaking generally. If there are twelve or more persons who wish to come together for this purpose it would be wiser to make two

---

[1] Op. cit., p. 24.

[2] 'The Bible and Higher Criticism': article by C. H. Dodd in *The Student World*, April, 1941, p. 127.

[3] E. H. Robertson's *Take and Read* (SCM Press, 1961) is a fuller treatment of group study. Mr Robertson has, like many others among us, learned from Mlle de Diétrich.

smaller groups, but the two leaders should work very closely together, and the two groups could meet at the end of a period for mutual discussion, and the pooling of 'findings'. 'The value of our group work will depend ultimately on the seriousness of the personal study of the Bible and the prayer-life of each of its members.'[1]

This brings us to the use of this book for personal meditation. It provides an admirable basis for such a practice. Very often, especially for people who have very little time, one chapter will provide enough material for meditation for the better part of a week. The chapter could be read on Sunday, or at any rate at the week-end, and the various passages allotted to the following days, so that no time is wasted when one is in the press of daily work.

Some people are rather frightened by the very word 'meditation'; they think it is something rather difficult, and only suitable for people of a peculiar cast of mind, or who 'like that sort of thing'. This is of course right off the mark. The actual process is one we employ every day : whenever we think over some plan or project—like buying a present for someone, or planning a holiday, or seeing how to make the best use of an unexpected chance of a holiday abroad —we *think* about it; we turn it over in our minds; if this raises questions we either look up the subject in a book, or we ask a knowledgeable friend for advice. Finally, when we have seen clearly what we ought to do, or want to do, we *act* on it, and we carry out our resolve in our ordinary daily life. We have 'made' our meditation.

So it may be here with this subject of real freedom : as we try to follow this subject through the Bible, with the help of these clear and simple, but often deep reflections, we shall find a growing fascination in this line of thought, and the more concrete we can make it the better. Above all, as the author has already reminded us, such study should lead us to prayer, and be carried on in the spirit of prayer, and of obedience to the will of God, *here and now*. Then we

Discovering the Bible, p. 59.

shall find, more and more, that 'his service *is* perfect freedom'.

A medieval writer says that there are four steps in the spiritual life: Reading, meditation, prayer and contemplation. Together they form a 'ladder' between heaven and earth, 'having but few steps, but reaching an immense distance'. Then he adds: 'Seek by reading, and you will find by meditation; knock in prayer, and it will be opened to you in contemplation.'

FOREWORD

I

IN CONTEMPORARY LANGUAGE the word 'liberty' is used in several different senses. But the main point is this: we need to know *from what* we are, or wish to be, liberated.

When a young man says 'I want to be free!' he usually means that he wants to do as he likes, that he wants to escape from the control of his parents or relatives, or from anyone who has authority over him—he means that he wants 'to live his own life'. This reminds us of the parable of the Prodigal Son, in which Jesus speaks of the younger son who claims his share in the inheritance due to him, leaves his home, and goes out into the world in search of adventure.[1] We shall see that the story of this 'bad boy' is really the story of the whole of humanity, which has left its home and its Father to seek for adventure, an adventure which has turned out rather badly.

When a mature man says: 'I want to be free!' as a rule he means that he is tired of his present situation: perhaps he is tired of his family ties and duties, perhaps of the monotony of his work. Then he begins to dream about *money*; money seems to him to be the key which would open the way to an easy life, in which he would be 'free'; that is, one in which he could 'escape' from his present life and all its obligations. He dreams of the pleasure of being freed from dependence upon others! of the delight of being his own master at last! what a relief to be released from other people for whom one is responsible, and be able to enjoy one's own existence!

[1] Luke 15.12.

For a prisoner, on the other hand, there is only one hour which counts: that of his 'release'; the moment when he will no longer be separated from the rest of mankind by insuperable barriers. Possibly sometimes he is a little afraid of this return to normal life, of the way in which his 'people' will receive him, of the unknown 'tomorrow'. And yet the nostalgia of liberty is there, and his whole being aches with longing for the arrival of the moment of release. The Bible says a great deal about 'captives', for they are a kind of symbol of human existence in its inexorable confinement between birth and death . . .

In a country 'occupied' by a foreign army, or in a country under colonial administration, to be 'free' means to get rid of the occupying power, to be free for self-government. Millions of men today are passionately longing for this kind of freedom. For this they are ready to shed their blood. We have had many illustrations of this in the recent history of Europe, Asia and Africa. A modern author has said: 'Men have never died well save for liberty: for then they have not wholly died.'[1] Camus reminds us, however, in this same passage, that there is no true liberty apart from *justice*.

Political liberty is a great thing. But history shows us that in itself it cannot make men truly free. The French Revolution inscribed the words 'Liberty, equality, fraternity' upon its monuments, and then imposed a reign of terror. The apprenticeship to liberty is long and difficult. In our own day we have come to realize that there is no true political liberty where there is neither economic freedom nor social justice.

What is the use of having a vote to a man who cannot find a decent house for his family? who is not free to choose his trade or profession? or who cannot give his children the education he desires? Probably that is why so many people today are indifferent to democratic liberty. This kind of liberty has not given them those other freedoms

[1] Camus, *L'homme révolté*, p. 360.

which alone will enable them to be 'persons' in the full sense of the word. When men think only about their own personal interests, or when they are only concerned about the interests of their own class, or party, or race, or country —there can be neither justice nor liberty.

To be free men implies certain exterior conditions, but also, and much more, certain interior conditions: self-mastery and the power to devote oneself to others, the sense of belonging to the whole family of man.

II

The ancient Greeks had already discovered this. They attached a great deal of importance to the liberty of the citizen: the free man, with his duties and his rights. On the other hand, there was also the slave who was the pro-perty of his master, that is to say, strictly speaking, he was rather 'a thing' than a man. The philosopher Plato empha-sized chiefly the danger of a liberty which does not keep the laws; for him this meant first of all obedience to the civic authorities, respect for parents and for the 'elders'. He said that a country is on the verge of ruin when there is no respect for law, and that it is lost when it does not respect the given word, nor undertakings made in the sight of God; for then the will to power takes charge, and the land can only go down to destruction in ruin and misery. Individualism and anarchy brought the Greek democracies to ruin; this fact is a warning for the democracies of every age.

For the Greek philosophers liberty was one of the most precious gifts that man can possess, whether it be the liberty of the state or of the individual. Liberty consists in not being dependent upon others, and in being able to dis-pose freely of one's own person. A free man is one who 'does not fear any earthly master, and submits to God alone'. There are external conditions which do not depend upon ourselves; we must be sufficiently detached to accept them willingly as the will of God. It was thus that Socrates calmly accepted death. Thus in this way even a slave or a prisoner can be inwardly free. Such was the Stoic Epictetus in the first century of our era; he was the slave of a brutal master and it is said that one day his master was torturing him by twisting his leg. Epictetus said calmly: 'You'll break my leg'; and when this had happened he said simply: 'I told you so.' He insisted on believing that everything which happened to him was an expression of the will of God. His liberty consisted in this act and attitude of acceptance. He confessed that the most difficult thing for him was to be liberated from his fear of death. Toward the end of his life he complained sadly: 'Show me a sick man who is still happy; in danger and happy; in exile and happy; one for whom everything goes wrong and yet he is happy! I want to see a real Stoic. But you cannot show me one who is perfect. Grant this grace to an old man, show me this miracle that I have never seen!'

The final word of Greek philosophy is this effort to achieve freedom by an attitude of complete detachment from life and from death. Epictetus records his own defeat. But is not this very 'detachment', in itself, a very negative attitude towards life?

In our own day we see a great religion, that of Islam, preaching a fatalism which has some relation with the fatalism of the ancient world: all that happens is the will of Allah, and all that man can, and should do, is to submit.

Fifty years ago many people were inclined to deny human liberty in the name of scientific determinism. Since then philosophy has evolved. Today it is psychology which takes the machinery of human nature to pieces as one would dismantle a machine. We are the product of heredity or of our environment, or of our temperament. Pushed to the extreme limit such theories destroy all our moral responsibility, but very few people go so far as that.

And because men have often made a bad use of what they called their 'liberty', we see today those who are tempted to renounce this liberty : the success of dictatorship in politics is simply due to the fact that people are so tired of the effort to rule themselves that they willingly hand over their responsibilities to someone who is stronger than they are. And because dictators are almost always people who believe in no one save themselves : who depend on their *own* strength and their own wisdom, they can only maintain their régime by force. 'If God does not exist, then everything is permitted.' This famous saying from a hero in one of Dostoevsky's works has been cruelly verified in history in men like Hitler and Stalin.

Where God does not reign, man finishes by regarding himself as a god. The demon of power holds him in its grip.

We live in a time when some peoples are clamouring passionately for liberty, while others ignore it because they are disillusioned.

In both cases two things have been forgotten : first of all, that liberty is never an end in itself. We are liberated *from something* and *for something*. The true question is this : '*From what* do you want to be liberated? and *for what*?'

Secondly, exterior liberty—political or material—is nothing without an interior liberty; it can only lead to new forms of slavery.

III

The Bible comes to us with a clear message, which is not that of the politicians, nor of the psychologists, nor of the philosophers. It proclaims the 'glorious liberty of the children of God'. It does not merely proclaim this : for in the centre of the Bible there stands a Man, *the only free man who has ever lived* : his name is Jesus.

All through the Bible, when a man listens to God, commits his life to his Word, we see him gaining an astonishing liberty with regard to the people and events of his own time: it is the liberty of the prophet, the liberty of the apostle. People may kill such men but they cannot make them dumb. Centuries later they speak to us still.

But we see immediately that the Bible means by 'liberty' something very different from the meaning given by most people to the word. It knows very well that there is no absolute liberty for human beings. Man has only the choice between two masters: God, or the one whom Jesus calls the 'Prince of this world'.[1]

Well, if this be so, can we still speak of 'liberty' at all? The Bible says 'Yes', because man has been created *by God* and *for God*. It is in finding God, or rather, in being found by God, that man finds his true self, and in so doing finds the experience of liberty. It is very paradoxical but it is true. And every Christian who has begun to expose himself to the action of Christ knows it: to live 'in Christ' is to grow in liberty, a liberty which no one can take from us.

When the psychologists tell us that we are prisoners of all kinds of forces which make us act in one way rather than in another, they are certainly not wholly wrong. The past of my parents and my own past have made me what I am. All this weighs upon me, and I can only change myself within certain limits. I am the prisoner of my self-centredness, of my desires, or of my pride. But there is someone who can transform my life: his name is Jesus Christ.

The story of the Prodigal Son began with the first human couple when they wanted to rule their own lives, to 'be as gods'. The man and the woman shut themselves out of the Paradise of God. They wanted to be 'free', and now we see them slaves of all the forces which work havoc in our human hearts, and divide men from one another. The great and tragic adventure of humanity has begun: envy and murder are born in the heart of man.

[1] John 12.31; 14.30.

And in order that we may rediscover our true home, and with it true liberty, God himself has to come down into this prison of humanity and by a miracle of love break down the bars of our prison, not from without but from within. That is the story of Jesus Christ: he takes upon himself our condition as man; he alone is free, and he alone is the sole liberator.

The great deliverance which the New Testament proclaims is deliverance from sin and death. That is the 'captivity' *par excellence*, the fundamental slavery of which all other forms of slavery are only the signs or the consequences.

The Old Testament, with its message of partial and partly material deliverances, proclaims the greater deliverance which is to come.

All down the centuries, with a mysterious patience, God waits for the final return of his prodigal children. He himself, of his own free choice, makes the great adventure of liberty. For he does not want 'slaves' but 'sons', 'friends', who will respond freely to his love, who will co-operate freely with his purpose of salvation for the whole of mankind. And he makes every soul won back by his Son, every child of the Kingdom, a 'saviour', who in his turn goes forth to proclaim to his brothers the one and only secret of true liberty.

PART ONE

MOVING TOWARDS LIBERTY

I

THE LOST LIBERTY

Read Genesis: chapters 1-3; 4.1-16

THE FIRST CHAPTERS of Genesis tell us the story of the Creation. God creates light, he creates heaven and the earth, the plants and the animals. 'And God saw that it was good.' Then God creates man and woman 'in his image'. He makes them his representatives upon the earth; he tells them to rule it in his name: 'Be fruitful, and multiply, and replenish the earth and subdue it; and have dominion over the fish of the sea, and over the fowl of the air, and over every living thing that moveth upon the earth.'[1]

Thus God establishes between the first human couple a *personal relationship*. It is this relationship which distinguishes man from the animal creation: God speaks to him; God entrusts him with a responsibility. Thus God makes man a free being: man alone in all the creation can say 'yes' or 'no' to his Creator.

God creates man and woman: between them he establishes a living relation which is meant to reflect something of his own love: he gives them to each other; he calls them to be united to one another in a joyful confidence, without shame and without scruple.[2] On one point alone God limits this joyful liberty: there is a fruit of which human beings may not eat.[3]

What does this mean? It means that there is a sphere

[1] Gen. 1.16-28.   [2] Gen. 2.18-23.   [3] Gen. 2.15-17.

which is reserved to the Creator alone: he alone knows
what is good and evil: he alone knows all things. Man must
recognize and accept his limitations as a creature; it is in
obeying his vocation as *man*, in not trying to go beyond
it, that he will know true liberty, that he will be able to
taste the fruits of the Tree of Life.

But now the obedience of this first human community
is put to the test: they look at the forbidden fruit and long
for it. (Do you notice the attraction of forbidden fruit? . . .
which of us has not known it?)

The woman succumbs to the temptation first, and she
draws her husband after her. From the actual moment when
she begins to argue with the tempter (serpent) she is on a
dangerous and slippery slope. He insinuates a doubt into
her mind: 'Yea, hath God said? . . .' Then he suggests that
God is jealous of his power. If she and her husband eat of
this beautiful fruit they will be 'as gods'! They will be
free! They will be their own masters! After this they will
not have to render account of their actions to anyone![1]
(And still today men dream of this kind of liberty . . .) And
now, the thing is done: they have eaten the forbidden fruit.
Have they found liberty? No, they have *lost* it.

They hide from one another: *shame* has entered into
their lives. No longer can they be completely themselves.
They have lost the innocent joy of their mutual relationship.[2] They hide from God. They no longer live in his
presence with the confidence of children. And then (and
how we see ourselves here too!) each reproaches the
other: the man accuses his wife, and in so doing, God
himself ('the woman whom thou gavest'); the woman
accuses the serpent[3] . . . Both try to get rid of their responsibility.

Their free and open relationship has been broken. Each
has his own desires, secret thoughts which he does not express. Desire is born in the woman, the instinct of domina-
ation in the man. The one wants to attract, the other to

[1] Gen. 3.1-5.   [2] Gen. 3.6-7.   [3] Gen. 3.8-13.

dominate. It is no longer the act of free self-giving without any other thought at all.

They want to be masters of the world. And behold they are not even masters of themselves. Suffering, the struggle for existence, and solitude become their daily lot.[1]

What is God going to do? He accepts this new situation: he clothes the man and the woman in order to hide this nakedness which is no longer innocent; then he removes them from the 'Tree of Life'.[2] They were now under the signature of death. God only confirms that this fact has taken place, and from it he draws the inevitable conclusions.

A long, long pilgrimage upon earth will be necessary before the Son of God will come and reopen the way to the Tree of Life. We find this Tree on the last page of the Bible, this Tree whose leaves are 'for the healing of the nations'.

In the meantime the human community will mourn its lost liberty; it will wander about the ways of the earth, which are marked with the sign of sin and death.

God had made man to be 'over against' him in responsibility. He made woman to be the companion 'over against' the man. To them both he had entrusted the care of the created universe. In not accepting the destiny which God had given them, in wishing to be their own masters, these human beings have cut themselves off from God, and also from their neighbour. Henceforth they are like tops which spin round themselves; they twist and turn and knock against one another.

Humanity is going to become a world of spinning tops: each man thinks first of all of himself; little individual tops which prevent the creation of any real community. Big tops: one clan up in arms against the other; one power against another power. And all these turning round and round themselves in a closed circle. In detaching ourselves from God we have destroyed love; we have destroyed all true liberty in human relationships.

The Bible shows us the immediate consequences of the

[1] Gen. 3.14-19.　　　　[2] Gen. 3.22.

rupture in the story of Cain. Cain has not the love of God in his heart; he is jealous of his brother: 'Sin coucheth at the door.' Cain could however still resist the temptation, and God warns him; but Cain does not listen. He becomes the first murderer.[1] This liberty which was given to man to create love he uses to kill. But are men still concerned about liberty? Man has become the slave of his passions. His cleverest inventions become a means of killing his enemies still more efficiently.[2] War has entered into the history of man.

The first eleven chapters of Genesis show us how a humanity which turns away from God destroys itself. It also shows us how God in his mercy preserves a faithful remnant, like Enoch or Noah. It was said of each of these men that 'he walked with God'.[3] What a magnificent description of the 'righteous' man, of a man who is free: a man who walks with God!

Noah saved from the Flood is like a promise, a sign of liberations to come. And the little ark tossed on the waves which contains in itself the seed of a new world is like a symbol of the Church, the bearer of a message of resurrection and life.

The story of the Tower of Babel[4] shows us men building their first great city. They have learned how to make bricks; they are proud of their wisdom and their power. They want 'to make a name' for themselves by building a tower which will reach to heaven. This is the exaltation of a 'great power' which thinks it can do anything. But God 'confounded their language'. The greater the enterprise the greater its fall; for a kingdom divided against itself cannot stand.

What is going to become of this humanity, which, in losing God, has lost the meaning of its life and can do no more than tear itself to pieces?

Who will deliver it from this slavery?

The history of salvation begins with Abraham.

[1] Gen. 4.1-16. [2] Gen. 4.22-24. [3] Gen. 5.24; 6.9. [4] Gen. 11.1-9.

2

THE ANCESTOR

Read Genesis: chapters 12-22

BETWEEN THE YEARS 3,000 and 2,000 B.C. there already
existed, in the heart of Asia, on the banks of the Euphrates
(today in the country of Iraq), a great civilization: that
of ancient Babylon. The story of the Tower of Babel was
inspired by the greatness and the fall of Babylon.

It was not in one of these cities that God was going to
look for the man whom he will make the father of believers. Israel was always to remember that his ancestor was
'a wandering Aramean',[1] a simple shepherd, leading his
flocks from place to place.

Terah, the father of Abram,[2] belonged to these nomad
tribes. The Bible tells us that he left Ur of the Chaldees 'to
go into the land of Canaan; and they came unto Haran and
dwelt there'.[3] At Haran there was a sanctuary where the
nomads were in the habit of coming to worship the Moon-
god. It was there that the living God laid his hand upon
Abram. He spoke to him; and this word was both a command and a promise.

First of all there was the command: 'Get thee out of thy
country, and from thy kindred, and from thy father's house,
unto the land that I will show thee.'[4] The writer of the
Epistle to the Hebrews says: 'Abraham . . . went out, not
knowing whither he went.'[5]

[1] Deut. 26.5 (RV marg.).
[2] Remember that Abraham is the new name which God gave
Abram when he made a covenant with him: Gen. 17.5-8.
[3] Gen. 11.27-32.   [4] Gen. 12.1.   [5] Heb. 11.8.

The first step in the life of faith is this commitment without conditions to the service of the living God who calls us. We shall not really know that he is, save in obeying him, by taking seriously both his promises and his commands.

In order to enter into this life of faith we always have to 'leave' something 'behind'. For Abram it meant leaving his tribe, his customs, and his gods; this is the first condition which must be fulfilled if we are to be free for the service of the true God.

For some this will mean breaking with bad habits, with bad companions, with a certain way of thinking and living. For us all it means that we must break with our old proud Self; the outward breaks are only a first step towards liberation; the real chains are those which keep our hearts attached to earthly things rather than to God; and God alone can break them.

Jesus will not be less exacting than God was for Abram. *We* have to be ready to leave our families, and our property, and even our own life, to follow him.[1]

Thus when Abram leaves his country, alone with his own small family, to begin the great adventure of faith, he becomes a 'sign' for the believers of all ages. He becomes the 'Father of the faithful'.[2] He believes the promises of God and ventures everything on his word. This is the first step towards liberation.

But can we speak here of 'liberation'? It looks rather as though all that Abram has done is to change masters?

Well, in one sense this is true. We have seen that it is the vocation of man to live in a trustful relation with God, and that his liberty consists in the joyful acceptance of this relationship. In breaking this relation, man has become the slave of the idols which he has made for himself, in order to replace the absent God. He will only rediscover his primary vocation by changing his master, by a humble return to his God. He needs to learn obedience, and this

[1] Luke 9.23-25; 57-60.   [2] Isa. 51.2.

obedience will become his liberty and his joy; but this will not be an obedience without conflict and suffering; for we are part of a world which is in rebellion against God; long and hard is the way of return for the prodigal children.

Was it not once said of our Lord Jesus Christ himself that he 'learned obedience by the things which he suffered'?[1]

Abram went out without knowing where he was going. But God knew that this story of a Bedouin of another age would lead to Jesus Christ, in whom all the promises made to Abraham will find their fulfilment; in whom we shall rediscover our lost liberty in its fulness and joy.

For the command to 'leave all' is accompanied by a magnificent promise: 'I will make of thee a great nation, and I will bless thee, and make thy name great, and be thou a blessing: and I will bless them that bless thee, and him that curseth thee will I curse: and in thee shall all the families of the earth be blessed.'[2]

What an amazing promise to give to a man who has no children! It is a promise which extends from the limits of the particular tribe to which he is going to give birth, right out to the whole world. Is it not impressive to note that more than four thousand years since this promise was made, the three most important religions of the world, that of the Jews, the Christians, and the Muslims, all claim Abraham as their common ancestor?

Certainly we have to remind ourselves of the distinction made by Jesus between the children of Abram 'according to the flesh' and his descendants 'according to faith'.[3] God alone knows who are his true children; but does not their number grow from age to age? does it not extend today, by the grace of God, to all the nations of the earth?

The 'Covenant' is going to play a great part in the whole history of Israel: it is by this that God is going to prepare

[1] Heb. 5.8-9.   [2] Gen. 12.2-3; cf. 15.4-6; 17.5; 22.15-18.
[3] John 8.39-45, 52-58.

the way for the restoration of the relationship with him which had been broken by the Fall.

The word 'covenant' denotes a contract, that is to say, a reciprocal pledge. But this covenant has something very special about it, because here the initiative comes wholly from God. It is *he* who takes the first step: it is he who pledges himself to Abraham and his posterity. On the other hand, Abram's response is the free response of faith. 'And he believed in the Lord and he counted it to him for righteousness.'[1] That is to say: God regards as 'righteous' one who trusts in him, who expects everything from him.

And now we see a mysterious ceremony.[2] Abram is preparing a sacrifice; he divides the animals into two parts. According to an ancient rite, when a solemn covenant was made, the two contracting parties passed through the animals which lay on either side of their path; that was intended to mean: 'If I break my word, may it be unto me as it is with these animals.' And behold when night fell Abram saw a flaming torch passing between the 'pieces' of the animals on the ground. This fire symbolized God's side of the covenant. Thus God in his mercy pledges himself to Abram and to all his descendants. He himself will restore the relation with himself which we had broken by our revolt.

We shall never fully comprehend the significance and the extent of this act of love, save in Jesus Christ. For God, in the person of his Son, will take upon himself upon the Cross the chastisement which the broken covenant requires. He will pass through death in order to give us back our true life, and the glorious freedom of the children of God.

The life of Abraham is a long apprenticeship to the life of faith. He does not suddenly become a free man. He is afraid of death to the point of committing a great act of cowardice, and of allowing his wife to be at the mercy of the capricious whims of Pharaoh; but God was watching and he saved Sarah.[3] Abram has doubts of the promises of God,

---

[1] Gen. 15.6.   [2] Gen. 15.7-17.   [3] Gen. 12.10-16; cf. Gen. 20.

and thinks it is safer to have his son Ishmael rather than to wait for the legitimate son whom God has promised; he tries to give a little 'push' on his own account, in order to make the fulfilment of God's purpose a little easier.[1] After all God does expect him to believe such impossible things!

On the other hand, Abram is a true believer who loves God and wants to obey him. He is generous and noble in his attitude towards Lot, and remarkably detached from the things of this world. He welcomes some unknown guests with generous hospitality and finds that he has received angels, and indeed more than that: God himself.[2]

Then his faith and his love are put to the extreme test: God asks him to give back to him the son of the Promise, Isaac, the child so long awaited, so tenderly loved. What is Abram going to do? Does not God, in asking for this sacrifice, cancel all his own promises?

Abraham does not argue. For a second time he sets out; he obeys quite simply; but how hard was this second departure in faith (not knowing whither he went). The story of these three days of the journey of the father and child towards Mount Moriah are some of the most harrowing pages in the whole of the Bible. They foreshadow another three days' journey, when the Son 'sets his face to go to Jerusalem'.[3]

Here the faith of Abraham is tried as by fire. His son was given back to him, says the writer of the Epistle to the Hebrews, by a kind of resurrection.[4]

Yes, this man loved God; he loved him above all things; he loved him more than his own life; more than this child who was more precious to him than his own self. And God loved him. Future generations called him the 'friend of God'.[5] It was this 'friendship which made him the Father of Believers (the faithful)'. This Bedouin of the desert is the first traveller on the long journey of man toward true

---

[1] Gen. 16; cf. 17.5-21 : 18.11-15. [2] Gen. 13.1-13; 14.21-24.
[3] Luke 13.31-33. [4] Heb. 11.17-19.
[5] James 2.23; cf. II Chron. 20.7; Isa. 41.8-9.

liberty, which God gives to us when we give ourselves to him.

One day God will come down to us in Jesus, and will make himself our Friend and our Brother.

'Your father Abraham rejoiced to see my day; and he saw it and was glad.'[1]

3

A CAPTIVE PEOPLE FINDS LIBERTY

Read Exodus: chapters 1-4; 16; 19-20

IT IS AN interesting fact that the first great act of divine liberation for the people whom he had chosen for himself, is an act of political liberation. This act certainly has a deeper meaning than appears on the surface, as we shall see. But the Bible says that God had heard the cry of his oppressed people, and that he has had compassion upon them. So he comes down to deliver them.[2]

The God of the Bible is not a distant God, hidden in heaven. He is a God who sees and hears what is happening upon earth. Sometimes, for a long time he is silent; but sooner or later the oppressors will have to render an account to him; no cry for deliverance is ever forgotten.

Israel would always remember that God had delivered her from the bondage of Egypt by his almighty hand: it is to the living God, who entered one day into her history, that she gave her faith and her love.

The tribes who had sought refuge in Egypt had not always been oppressed. For them Egypt had been a place of refuge in time of famine. But their rapid growth in popula-

[1] John 8.56.   [2] Ex. 2.23-25; 3.7-8.

tion had caused the authorities to feel uneasy. A new dynasty came to the throne; the Pharaohs requisitioned the Israelites for their building schemes and established a system of forced labour which became harsher and harsher as time went on. It was actual slavery, without the name.[1]

It was then that God raised up for them a liberator in the person of Moses.

This man Moses had been brought up at the Egyptian court; he was regarded as an Egyptian; he was a free man. But he heard men speaking of the sufferings of the people of his own race. He took part in a painful scene and revenged his Hebrew brother by killing the Egyptian; he hoped that no one had seen him doing it.[2]

This first intervention of Moses has two sides : good and bad. The good side is that he took the part of his unhappy brethren and its risks and perils. But it is not by murder that we fulfil the purpose of God. Moses gave way to anger: he was not yet ready for his mission. He still needed to learn true liberty in obedience to God. The consequences of his rash act recoiled upon himself and he was obliged to flee for his life. God led him to the humble work of a shepherd, which was the work of his forefathers, and Moses served an apprenticeship of forty years in the land of Midian.[3]

And then came the hour of revelation. God appeared to Moses as the God of his fathers, *his God*, the living God, 'Jahweh'. And God gave him his mission : to be the deliverer of his people. This time Moses had no desire to play the part of a liberator. He tried to find all sorts of excuses. But God still said : *Go!*[4]

When Moses appeared before Pharaoh he was a different person; he had no strength save that which God gave him. But because his strength came from God, and not from him-

[1] Ex. 1.8-14; cf. 5.5-18.   [2] Ex. 2.1-15.
[3] For this first episode in the life of Moses, read : Ex. 2; Acts 7.17-29; Heb. 11.23-26.
[4] Ex. 3; and 4.10-17.

self, he was perfectly master of himself; he was not afraid of anything; he was *free*.[1]

Moses had a hard struggle with the Pharaoh of Egypt; for the latter always took back his word when the danger was over . . . But there was a second conflict which was no less difficult: that which Moses had to wage with his own people, who were afraid to run the risks of liberty, and who preferred the 'flesh-pots' of Egypt, and servitude, to the privations of the desert.[2]

Thus this man who had left everything in order to give himself to the task of liberation found himself strangely alone. His faith opened a path through the sea and the desert, and he only just managed to persuade those whom he had delivered from slavery to follow him. Their hearts were not free from fear: fear of the enemy, fear for the morrow, fear of the sacrifices which might be asked of them. They were too little, too timid, for the great adventure which God had forced them to make. Their faith was not equal to his promises.

We should not judge them too hardly: we too cling tightly to our human forms of security, and do not dare to run the full risk of a liberty which stakes all upon God alone, for all our future days.

Why did God set these tribes free from the Egyptian yoke? He says clearly that it was in order that they should *serve him*. 'And thou shalt say unto Pharaoh, Thus saith the Lord, Israel is my son, my firstborn . . . Let my son go that he may serve me.'[3] God willed to create a people for himself whose whole life would bear the marks of him who had redeemed them; whose whole life should be for his glory; a people in the midst of the nations which would be a living witness to the faithfulness, the liberty, of their God. Thus the political liberation is only a step towards a higher liberty; its aim is not in itself. What matters is to build a nation whose liberty will be founded entirely upon obedience to God.

[1] Ex. 5 ff; cf. Heb. 11.27.   [2] Ex. 16.3; cf. 17.1-4.   [3] Ex. 4.22

Like all true liberty it has its own laws. God gave them at Sinai. He taught his people all that they ought not to do on pain of falling back into a worse form of slavery than the first. For it was in dependence upon God that Israel had found her life; and in rediscovering God, Israel rediscovered his neighbour, his brother. God does not call isolated individuals, he creates a community, a people.

The foundation of the life of Israel is faith in the living God.[1]

The first liberation which it had to experience was to learn to be set free from idols. All round Israel in Canaan there lived idolatrous peoples; people who worshipped gods who were often cruel, to the extreme of demanding human sacrifice; they were pagans who practised sorcery and magic; who lived in continual fear of demons. All that was forbidden to Israel: the Saviour-God who had delivered his people from servitude in Egypt also intends to set them free from servitude to idols. And his people were slow to understand: Moses had hardly left them for a moment when they began making a golden calf![2]

But idols are not only made of wood and metal: our particular 'idol' has a great many names; it may be love of money, or success, or reputation. Everything which takes the place of God in our hearts, is an idol. Israel was to know all these dazzling illusions of power and glory.

After belief in the One God the Decalogue mentions the Sabbath. Why is so much importance attached to the day of rest? Does this directly concern the life of faith? Work is part of the normal life of every human being. 'If a man will not work, neither shall he eat', says St Paul. But God the Creator who has made both day and night in order that man may both work and rest[3] has set apart one day in seven in order that on that day we may remember God, may leave for a moment all the toil and care for our daily bread, in order to meditate upon the divine rest into which one day we shall enter.

[1] Ex. 20.1-7; cf. Deut. 5.1-11.   [2] Ex. 32.   [3] Ps. 104.23.

B

This 'slowing-down' of the pace of life at regular intervals should help us to preserve our interior liberty, with regard to the things of this world which passes away. At the same time it is a social law which secures a period of freedom for all who serve others, and for the animals as well.[1]

What are the other laws which condition the life of the tribe?[2] First of all, reverence for parents; then, conjugal fidelity; respect for the life and property of others; then, great regard for truth ('false witness' is severely punished). For the anger which leads to murder, the envy which fills the heart with greedy desire, are serious forms of slavery which rob man of his self-mastery, plunge him into lying, and destroy confidence between persons.

The Law of Moses contains a series of *social* laws. God watches with particular care over those who are unable to stand up for their own rights: the poor, the widow, the orphan and the foreigner.[3] For they too should be able to live in a way which will not rob them of their liberty, by falling into destitution or slavery. And all this is summed up in the words: 'Thou shalt love thy neighbour as thyself.'[4]

Thus the laws that God gave to his people were not the commandments of a harsh, tyrannical master; what God wills, is to establish loyal, generous, true, relations between those who belong to his people; this will establish justice and peace, and thus lead to liberty.

It is important to note that no healthy political and social life can exist where these elementary laws of life are not respected.

When Israel violated them once more she fell into slavery; once more she experienced oppression; first of all from within, and later, from without, through invasion.

[1] Ex. 20.8-11; 23-12.   [2] Ex. 20.12-17 and chapters 21-23.
[3] Ex. 22.21-27; 23.1-11.   [4] Lev. 19.17-18.

4

THE PROPHET CONFRONTS THE KING

NOW WE LEAP over several centuries. Israel is now settled in Canaan. She has asked God for a king and God has given her one. The king is the 'Anointed of the Lord'; it is his mission to lead the people in the name of God, and to fight against idolatry. But very often the kings fail in their mission. The priests, too, allow themselves to be drawn away into idolatry. When this happens, God raises up a new kind of man, a man after his own heart, a man who will be his mouth: the Prophet.

At the outset we must recognize the fact that there were true prophets and false prophets. The false prophet is the man who tells the people what they want to hear; he feeds on 'dreams'; he takes his own words for the word of God:

> Thus saith the Lord of hosts concerning the prophets, Hearken not unto the words of the prophets that prophesy unto you; they teach you vanity: they speak a vision of their own heart, and not out of the mouth of the Lord. They say continually unto them that despise the word of the Lord, The Lord hath said, Ye shall have peace: and unto everyone that walketh in the stubbornness of his own heart they say, No evil shall come upon you.[1]

The true prophet is bound by the word of God. It burns him like a fire. It is like a 'hammer that breaketh the rock in pieces'. The man who perceives this cannot be silent, even though it may cost him his life.[2]

The prophets of Israel were great men. In hours of crisis they suddenly emerge with an authentic word from God; they tell the truth: to kings, to priests, to magistrates, and

---

[1] Jer. 23.16-17. RV marg.   [2] Jer. 23.29 and 20.7-9.

to all who have betrayed their trust. They are like the living conscience of their people at a moment when all other
voices are silent. But what they say and what they do they
say and do in the power of God. This is the source of their
amazing freedom in dealing with men and with circumstances. They are a living illustration of the fact that it is
the Word of God which makes 'men'.

Now let us listen to some of them.

1. *David and Nathan.* Read II Samuel, chapters 7; 11;
12.1-25.

King David was a king 'according to God's own heart'.
He took his royal vocation seriously; he feared God, and it
was in the name of the Lord that he ruled and served his
people. His guide and counsellor was Nathan, the Man of
God.

But this king also had terrible weaknesses. For instance,
at one time he envied the wife of one of his army officers,
and he took her while her husband was away on duty. The
first sin brought another in its train. The king did not know
how to extricate himself from the net in which he was
caught. Finally, he took the desperate course of planning
that his faithful servant should be killed in battle. It was
a murder in disguise. David, powerful as he was, was not
a free man.

Then God sent Nathan to him. Nathan told him a story
about a poor man who had nothing save one little ewe
lamb. Close to him there lived a rich man. And he took the
poor man's lamb away from him for himself. David was
indignant; he said to Nathan: 'As the Lord liveth, the man
that hath done this is worthy of death!' Then Nathan
turned on David, saying: *'Thou art the man!'*

It does not take a great deal of courage to denounce sin
in a general way, for no one feels that this applies to them,
or that their sin has been laid bare. But it takes a great deal
of courage to go to a man, to speak to him face to face,
and to say: *'You* have done this or that, and it is wrong.'

It costs still more if this man is a person of authority, and indeed the ruler of the country.

We have an instance of this in our own day. Under the Third Reich one day Pastor Niemöller went to see Hitler, in order to say to him : 'You are doing wrong.' Hitler never forgave him. He made Niemöller his 'personal prisoner', and to the end he refused to release him.

David was a believer : he accepted the divine judgment through the mouth of Nathan. Nathan told him that he would be forgiven, but that the child of his adultery would die.

David prayed desperately for the child's life. But God did not grant his prayer. Then the king accepted the chastisement as a believer should do. And by this humble acceptance he was set free from his sin. When God pardons he does it altogether. Bathsheba bore a second son, who would inherit the throne of David; of him it was said *God loved him*. And David entrusted this son to the care of the prophet Nathan. God alone can thus set us free from our guilty past, and allow anyone who truly repents to start a new life.

The story of David and Nathan shows us two things : the rôle of the man of God is to be like the living conscience of a great king. He proclaims the promises of God.[1] But when the king commits a sin he dares to tell him the whole truth. And the other side of the story shows the attitude of the king, who has the courage to admit his sin, and to accept God's judgment upon it; although he had momentarily given way to his passions, he recognizes the power of the word of God, which condemns the sin, and sets the repentant sinner free.

Happy the nation which possesses men of God who are sufficiently free to proclaim the truth which needs to be said to leaders who are willing to listen to the message.

2. *Ahab and the Prophets*. Read I Kings 16.29 to 19.20; chapters 21; 22.

[1] cf. II Sam. 7.

The story of Ahab presents us with a very different instance: it belongs to the long line of those whom the Bible calls the 'bad' kings, the kings who 'did that which was evil in the sight of the Lord'. Ahab, unfortunately, had married a pagan princess who was to be at all times his bad genius, his 'demon'. She brought with her her gods, her priests, her prophets of Baal, and Ahab, doubtless in order to give her pleasure, worshipped her idols.

Ahab was, above all, a weak man. He was afraid of the prophets of God, because he knew that when God spoke through them what they foretold *always happened*. Sometimes he consulted them; but in the end the opinions of Jezebel always swept him along with her, and she was implacably hostile to Elijah.

Elijah was a man whom God guided. No one knew *where* he would turn up! He would come and go unexpectedly: when he was sought, he disappeared. Then unexpectedly he would suddenly reappear in some other place. This exterior liberty was like a sign of the interior liberty which God gave him, which enabled him always to confront the trembling Ahab and the vindictive Jezebel with unabated courage.

Elijah announced that there would be a prolonged drought. The 'baals' were gods of the soil, and the priests of Jezebel wanted to persuade the people that it was these 'baals' who could control the rain. So a fierce conflict between them and Elijah ensued: 'Who is it makes the rain?' Elijah's life was threatened, and he had to flee, and God watched over him in his exile. Three years with no rain! The situation was tragic (chap. 18). Then Elijah reappeared. He threw down his challenge to the priests of Baal. It ended in a massacre. And the rain came.

But the anger of Jezebel, whose priests had been killed, was terrible. Once more Elijah had to flee for his life. This time he was tired of the struggle. He felt 'fed up'! He had had enough! Yet not only did God not abandon him, but he led him far away to the Mount of Horeb, the mount of revelation.[1] And there God revealed himself to him: not in the storm, nor in the fire, but by 'a still small voice'. What a revelation for a violent man who had just slaughtered four hundred prophets of Baal! And God taught Elijah something else as well: that he was not, as he thought, the only faithful prophet: there were seven thousand others who had not bowed their knees to Baal!

And here is another striking story.[2] Ahab envied the vineyard of Naboth because he wanted to make it into a 'garden of herbs'; the king offered money for it. But Naboth refused: he was a free man and this vineyard had belonged to his forefathers; he had no intention of giving it up. To every true Israelite the land he inherited from his ancestors was sacred: it was a little portion of the promised land which God had given to his forefathers, which was handed down from one generation to another.

Ahab went back to his palace 'heavy and displeased'. (He was often 'heavy and displeased' cf. 20.43.) It is characteristic of a man who is the slave of his desires, of his passing whims, of a man who is *not 'free'*, to be suspicious and 'difficult'.

Once more his 'demon' intervened in the person of Jezebel. And so we have the tragic story of the murder of Naboth. The murder was given the superficial appearance of legality; the 'elders' and the magistrates played the horrible farce which Jezebel had suggested. They too were not free men; they allowed themselves to be bought.

But there was one man who was free: the prophet Elijah once more confronted Ahab. And the king exclaimed: 'Hast thou found me, O mine enemy?' And Elijah answered: 'I have found thee because thou hast sold thyself to do that which is evil in the sight of the Lord . . .' This time Ahab had over-reached himself, and the judgment of God was pronounced: 'the dogs which have licked the blood of Naboth will lick the blood of Jezebel'.[3] The

---

[1] I Kings 19.8, Mt Sinai.   [2] I Kings 21.
[3] I Kings 21.23; cf. II Kings 9.30-37.

justice of God will act where human justice has failed.

We have one last sight of Ahab confronted by a prophet.[1] The King of Judah had joined the King of Israel to oppose Syria. But the King Jehoshaphat, unlike Ahab, was a god-fearing monarch; he insisted that, first of all, they must consult the prophets. They all encouraged the two kings to go to war. But Jehoshaphat was still uneasy. Ahab then admitted: 'there is yet one man by whom we may inquire of the Lord, Micaiah the son of Imlah: but I hate him, for he doth not prophesy good concerning me but evil'.

A messenger was sent to summon Micaiah who spoke thus to him: 'Behold . . . the words of the prophets declare good unto the king with one mouth: let thy word, I pray thee, be like the word of one of them, and speak thou good!'

But Micaiah was a true man of God, a free man, who could not be 'bought': 'As the Lord liveth', he said, 'what the Lord saith unto me, that will I speak!'

Ahab adjured Micaiah to speak the truth. And then he put him in prison for having done so. To the end of his life Ahab was a cowardly, deceitful man: he disguised himself in order to escape the attack of those who were lying in wait for him. But when God has spoken nothing can stop the judgment of God. Ahab died on the field of battle, and his army was defeated.

But no threats could kill Elijah, the man of God. With the new reign the struggle began again. Once more Elijah was a messenger of death. He always remained 'free' until God 'took him'.[2] What does this 'assumption' mean? In a humanity enslaved by its false gods Elijah arose as the breaker of idols, acting in the power of the Living God.

But there is another captivity: that which condemns every human being to death. The mysterious story of the 'translation' of Elijah is intended to proclaim the truth that there will be a final deliverance—that a day will come when death itself will be conquered.

[1] I Kings 22.   [2] II Kings 1 and 2.

5

THE SHEPHERD OF TEKOA

Read the Book of Amos; especially ch. 2. 6 to ch. 8
(inclusive)

TO THE EAST of Jerusalem stretch the arid mountains of
Judaea. Here the people used to live by breeding desert
sheep and by the cultivation of sycomore trees. The Bible
tells us that the King Uzziah, or Azariah, had cisterns made
in this desert in order to give water to the flocks of sheep,
'for he had much cattle'.[1] To the north lay the more fertile
plains of the Northern Kingdom, the Kingdom of Israel.
Doubtless Amos often went there to sell his wool and his
fruit.

About 750 B.C the two kingdoms both seemed to be very
prosperous. Uzziah had defeated the Philistines to the south;
'and his name spread abroad even to the entering in of
Egypt . . . for he waxed exceeding strong'. The King of
Israel, Jeroboam II, had also extended his frontiers to the
north, as far as Damascus. His reign would now be described as a 'period of economic expansion'; trade was going
very well. From the political point of view, he was a great
king. From the human point of view, there was nothing to
suggest that catastrophe was at hand. In point of fact, less
than forty years later the Kingdom of Israel was to disappear from the map of the Middle East.[2]

Two men alone saw the approaching storm : the prophet
Amos and the prophet Hosea; but no one believed them.

Who was Amos? He was not a learned man; he was not
even a townsman, one of those who are 'up in politics'. He

[1] II Chron. 26.10. [2] Fall of Samaria, 722 B.C.

was not even a 'prophet', in the technical sense of the word.
(For at that time there were 'schools of the prophets', whose
task it was to give oracles upon events.) No, Amos was simply a 'man of God', one of those men whom God takes hold
of where he chooses, and invests them with his power, in
order that men may hear his Word.

> 'Then answered Amos and said to Amaziah, I was no
> prophet, neither was I a prophet's son; but I was an herd-
> man and a dresser of sycomore trees: and the Lord took
> me from following the flock, and the Lord said unto me:
> Go, prophesy unto my people Israel.'[1]

Amos was a man of God who had grown up in solitude;
free as the wind of the desert; when the Spirit of God
breathed upon him he went wherever God told him to go.

The desert had moulded the character of Amos. He had
had to fight against nature in its most austere and savage
form; the life of a shepherd was not at all easy; he had to
search for pasture for his animals, and he also had to find
water for them; he had to defend them against wild beasts
and against robbers. The shepherd had to watch through
long silent nights; he knew that the wild beast which is out
hunting moves silently; and when the lion roars it means
that he has already laid hold of his prey; if the bird fall into
the net it is because there is a trap there.

And now, behold, the wrath of God is sounding in the
ears of Amos like the voice of a roaring lion. The holy God
has spoken, and he must obey.[2]

The destruction of the Kingdom of Israel has already
been decided!

How then did this certainty take hold of Amos, the shepherd of Tekoa?

In every authentic vocation there is a mystery, known
to no one, save God: he speaks to the heart of a man, and
all that this man can do is to obey. The prophet is a man
who is bound by the word of God:

[1] Amos 7.14-15.   [2] Amos 3.3-8.

'The lion hath roared, who will not fear?
The Lord God hath spoken, who can but prophesy?'[1]

But the divine inspiration does not act in a magical way.
God had opened the mind and heart of Amos to his law, to
his revelation, as it had already been given to his fathers.
The God who speaks by the mouth of Amos is the one holy
God proclaimed by Moses; the God who had delivered Israel
from the yoke of Egypt,[2] and who had just given them
victory over the Syrians; a God who is merciful to all who
repent, terrible in his judgments; a God who cannot endure
idolatry, who hates hypocrisy and lying; a righteous God,
the one who is for ever on the side of the oppressed, as
their defender.

The first conviction which God impressed upon the heart
of Amos was this: that it is he, Jahweh, who controls human
history. Nothing happens apart from his will. He has already spoken in the thunder and lightning of Sinai. Today
he still speaks. He warns his people by earthquakes and
famines, by the locusts who devour the grain. But all these
warnings have been in vain : the people have not returned
to him from their bad ways! 'yet have you not returned
unto me, saith the Lord'.[3] Behold the day of the Lord is at
hand! war and famine are at the gates of the city! this day
of the Lord will be a day of darkness and anguish : men will
creep about the doomed city—full of corpses—like shadows. None will dare to 'mention the name of the Lord'.[4]

What were the crimes which the people had committed?
Here we note with what precision the prophet enumerates
the vices which ruin a nation. He had been at Samaria; he
stopped at the market place and watched the traders;[5] he
listened to the sentences pronounced by the magistrates at
the gates of the city; he saw the luxury of the palaces and
the misery of the poor;[6] he stood outside the sanctuary and
watched the crowds worshipping the golden calf; he was

---

[1] Amos 3.8.   [2] Amos 2.10.   [3] Amos 4.6-12.
[4] Amos 5.18-20; 6.8-11.   [5] Amos 2.6; cf. 5.7, 10-12; 6.12.
[6] Amos 2.6-8; 4.1-4; 6.1-7.

present at religious festivals which were orgies and banquets pure and simple.[1]

This man *knows what he is talking about.* God has not only opened his eyes to the meaning of his Word, but *he has also opened his eyes to understand the world.* Amos sees this world, which henceforth he sees in the light of the Word of God, as God sees it. This display of luxury and taste does not dazzle him; these religious feasts do not impress him; the royal power which sanctions them does not terrify him.

For it is *God* who controls history, and not Jeroboam II. And in the heart of the prophet there burns the holy wrath of God. At the heart of Samaria the Lion of Juda roars. In the streets of Bethel there rises the wailing chant:

'The virgin of Israel is fallen, she will rise no more, she lieth forsaken . . .'[2]

The larger number of the poems of Amos are rhythmical poems; slow chants like those which are sung for the dead.

The crimes are denounced one by one. Every pretext is taken away. To those who claimed that the Covenant would give them security God replies:

'You only have I known of all the families of the earth, therefore I will visit upon you all your iniquities'.[3]

It is because God had liberated this people, had revealed himself to her, and had shown her mercy, times without number, that Israel is now without excuse. She has not 'come back'. An hour strikes when the terrible words re-echo: 'Too late!' The sentence has been pronounced.

The Assyrian has already spread his net. Israel has already been caught in the net of the fowler. Already the hour of massacre, of deportation is near. The people which did not know how to use its liberty is about to fall back into slavery. It is 'ripe for its end.'[4]

The mission of Amos has a very precise meaning: for the last time to call the kingdom of Israel to repentance; to re-

[1] Amos 3.14; 4.4-5; 5.21-26; cf. I Kings 12.26-32.
[2] Amos 5.2.   [3] Amos 3.2.   [4] Amos 8.2; cf. 5.25-27.

call it to its vocation to be the People of God, with all the responsibility that this vocation implies; and to proclaim to it the imminent punishment : exile.

In this sense the vocation of the prophet is unique : God reveals to him his own purposes.[1]

But the way in which Amos denounces the *causes of the corruption of the nation* contains a warning which is valid for all nations. With prosperity Israel became in fact enslaved to the power of money; the vices of civilization, drunkenness, prostitution, have destroyed this people which was previously simple and unpolished. Formerly a people of shepherds, without separate classes, Israel now knows the extremes of great luxury and great poverty and misery. The women set the example : they lead their husbands to drink; they are hard on the poor who knock at the door; like the fat cattle of the Mesopotamian plains, they think of nothing save of enjoying themselves and getting fat.[2] When woman loses her dignity as woman, society soon rots. That was the case with Samaria.

Above all there is one word which is continually on the lips of Amos : righteousness (justice). There is no longer any justice in the land. The judges let themselves be bought. That also is a sign of the decadence of a nation; and especially of a nation which had received the Law from God himself.

For all these corruptions spring from one sin, which lies at the root of all the others : Israel had ceased to believe in the living God. Israel believed in money, pleasure, success.

And when the prophet raised his voice, immediately he met a priest of the royal sanctuary who tried to silence this voice, which was so unwelcome : 'O thou seer, go, flee thee away into the land of Judah, and there eat bread and prophesy there : but prophesy not any more at Bethel : for it is the king's sanctuary and it is a royal house.' In modern language this means : 'What have you got to do with *us*, you street-preacher? Anyhow you don't belong to us! Go

[1] Amos 3.7.   [2] Amos 4.1.

home! *We* are good citizens, in the pay of the king! Go and earn your keep wherever you like—but leave us alone!'

But Amos did not cease to speak. For he was the kind of man who is free, free because he is commissioned by God.

A nation is very sick, a government is very weak, when neither the one nor the other can bear to be told the truth. A heavy silence falls because 'the times are bad'. Thus Amos still says to us: young men and women are still dying of thirst. Still people have a hunger and thirst to 'hear the words of the Lord'[1] but they wander all over the world and do not find it.

Is this God's final word? The conclusion of the book tells us that God's silence will not last for ever. When the fire of judgment has done its work a 'remnant' will remain, and will return, purified and liberated. By the test of trial God will restore that which he had broken.

And the word of the desert prophet whose voice had so long been silent will resound in men's hearts as a *word of God*, a word of judgment and a word of liberation—a word which is strong and encouraging. It sounds like the wind of the desert, the roaring of the lion, and still has power to awaken us, after two thousand eight hundred years.

6

AN IRON PILLAR

Read Jeremiah : chapters 1; 2; 11.18; 12.6; 15.15-21; 20; 26; 27; 28; 34; 37; 38

A LITTLE MORE than a hundred years have elapsed since the prophecy of Amos and the destruction of the kingdom of Israel. Now the bell is about to toll for a second time,

[1] Amos 8.11-14.

this time for the little kingdom of Judah. It is about to fall under the assault of Babylon, as Israel fell before the attacks of Assyria.

The long career of Jeremiah[1] took place at a moment when empires rose and fell with startling swiftness. Judah was carried away like a wisp of straw in the whirlwind of the nations. Possibly it might have remained undisturbed, in its hidden fastness among the hills, had not its king thrown himself into the struggle. The result was the country came under the domination of Assyria and then under that of Egypt, and finally under the yoke of Babylon, in its last collapse.

In Jeremiah we see once more that liberty of judgment regarding events and persons which has already impressed us in Amos; but we know more of the cost of this liberty to the prophet. No one has described more impressively the conflicts of an apostle, save St Paul. Amos was a 'hard' or a 'tough' man—a voice crying in the wilderness. Jeremiah was a sensitive soul, and each prophecy cost him tears of blood; for he had to announce the destruction of that which he loved. He would have liked to have escaped from his mission, but it was impossible.

God, in his sovereign freedom, had placed his hand upon this man from his mother's womb, in order to make him a prophet unto the nations. With seeming cruelty, one by one, God broke all the bonds which would have prevented Jeremiah from being the voice of freedom in a world in chains.[2]

Little by little we watch the conflict which is to transform this tender plant into an 'iron pillar' and a 'brazen wall'.

[1] The Book of Jeremiah contains 52 chapters: we have selected those passages which lay stress upon his vocation, his conflicts, which became particularly severe after the death of Josiah (609 B.C.). Jeremiah witnessed the deportations of 598-7, and 586 B.C. He was in constant conflict with the priests at Jerusalem, who had taken refuge in a 'false peace', and with the successors of Josiah, whose policy of resistance he attacked. For the historical background, read II Kings, chapters 22-25.   [2] Jer. 1.5.

'Thou therefore gird up thy loins and arise
and speak unto them all that I command thee:
Be not dismayed at them, lest I dismay thee before them.
For behold I have made thee this day a defenced city,
and an iron pillar, and brazen walls, against the whole
   land,
against the kings of Judah, against the princes thereof,
against the priests thereof,
and against the people of the land.
And they shall fight against thee;
but they shall not prevail against thee: for I am with
   thee,
saith the Lord, to deliver thee.'[1]

This meant solitude, but it was to be solitude with God.
Through the love of Jeremiah for his people, it is the heart
of God, grieved beyond measure, which is pleading for the
return of the unbeliever, reminding him of the love of former days.[2]

God is going to impart to Jeremiah something of his own
love, of his own solitude, that of a lover who has been forsaken, of his own liberty. And it is this which will give to
Jeremiah's message an inimitable accent of suffering and
of truth; it is that which will make him a precursor, and
almost a foreshadowing of Jesus Christ.[3]

But he too has to 'learn obedience'; for that is the secret
of liberty. This man, who speaks so beautifully of the
sweetness of home life, will remain alone all his life.[4] Even
in his youth he will be chased out of his village by people
who seek to kill him; just as Jesus was chased out of Nazareth.[5]

This prisoner of the Lord is sometimes terribly exasper-
ated by his calling as a prophet. He even goes so far as to
curse the day he was born.[6] Is such a blasphemy permitted?
Yes, when a cry of this kind is directed to God himself.
For he who has left all for God is free to speak to him
about his troubles. And God in his mercy understands this

[1] Jer. 1.17-19 (RV).   [2] Jer. 2.2, 32.   [3] cf. Matt. 16.14.   [4] Jer. 16.2.
[5] Jer. 11.18-23; cf. Luke 4. 14-30.   [6] Jer. 15.10; 20.14-16.

revolt better than many apparent expressions of submission which come merely from the lips and not from the heart. For this is the complaint of the wounded warrior. And God knows well enough that he will start out again when he has to do so.

But how roughly God treats his servant!

'If you have run with men on foot, and they have tired you out, then how can you keep up with the horses?'[1]

In other words: 'What! you are complaining already! Wait till you see what is coming!'

Jeremiah complains of God's delays, for he threatens and then does not carry it out. Thus the bearer of his Word is exposed to the taunts of scoffers. Will not God execute vengeance? Is God, after all, like a 'deceitful brook'? (Wilt thou really disappoint me like a brook that runs dry? *Moffatt*.) And Jahweh replies: 'If you return to me I will take you back into my service.' There is never the least concession. But there is always a renewal of his Promise: 'I am with thee, to save thee, and to deliver thee, saith the Lord.'[2]

God only gives his prophet the bread of the strong: obedience without conditions. It is thus that he will serve his apprenticeship to true liberty.

'O Lord thou hast deceived me, and I was deceived: thou art stronger than I, and hast prevailed; I am become a laughing-stock all the day, everyone mocketh me. For as often as I speak, I cry out; I cry, Violence and spoil: because the word of the Lord is made a reproach unto me, and a derision, all the day. And if I say, I will not make mention of him, nor speak any more in his Name, then there is in mine heart as it were a burning fire shut up in my bones, and I am weary with forbearing, and I cannot contain. For I have heard the defaming of many, terror on every side. Denounce, and we will denounce him, say all my familiar friends, they that watch for my halting; peradventure he will be enticed, and we shall prevail against him and we shall take our revenge on him. But the Lord is with me, as

---

[1] Jer. 12.5 (Moffatt).   [2] Jer. 15.15-21.

a mighty one, and a terrible; therefore my persecutors shall stumble, and they shall not prevail : they shall be greatly ashamed, because they have not dealt wisely even with an everlasting dishonour which shall never be forgotten. But, O Lord of hosts, that triest the righteous, that seest the reins and the heart, let me see thy vengeance on them; for unto thee have I revealed my cause. Sing unto the Lord, Praise ye the Lord; for he hath delivered the soul of the needy from the hand of evil-doers.'[1]

Can one say of a man who speaks like this that he is more enslaved than free? Yes, that which keeps him in chains is the burning fire of the love and the truth of God.

Who is more free : one who knows fear and hatred and doubt and always finally triumphs over them by a miracle of grace?—or one who, never having been under fire, knows neither the temptations nor the suffering of the conflict?

It is in the liberty of his dialogue with God that Jeremiah gains the strength he needs to speak the truth to men. And as he confronts them, what firmness, daring, and calmness he shows. Look at him in the heart of the Temple in Jerusalem announcing the destruction of the Holy Place. He speaks ironically of those who think they are secure, saying: 'It is the Temple of Jahweh, the Temple of Jahweh! the Temple of Jahweh!'

But in reality they have made it a 'den of robbers'. It will be destroyed.[2] Nothing, neither threats nor beatings nor dungeon has any power to shake his resolution. 'It is the Lord who sent me . . .' 'As for myself, I am in your power; you can do with me as you think right and good.'[3]

Look at him again in conflict with the prophet Hananaiah. For a moment Jeremiah seems to give way to him. But God intervenes. And Jeremiah comes back: 'The wooden yoke you have broken, but I will replace it with an iron yoke . . .'[4]

---

[1] Jer. 20.7-13.
[2] Jer. 7. Ch. 26 refers to the same episode—cf. also ch. 20.1-6.
[3] Jer. 26.14.   [4] Jer. 28.

Look at him again during the siege of Jerusalem. King Zedekiah, in the hour of danger, had made a compact with all the people of Jerusalem, that they would liberate all their Hebrew slaves. But once the worst danger was over they all 'forced back into slavery' the slaves whom they had liberated—contrary to the law of God. Then God spoke by the mouth of his prophet: 'Since you would not obey me, and proclaim freedom, each to his brother and fellow, I now proclaim you free, says the Eternal—free to fall under the sword, the pestilence and the famine! I will make your fate a terror to every kingdom upon earth.'[1] Does the punishment seem out of proportion to the crime? No! for it concerns men and their liberty; and the given word; the law of God, is at stake.

Is there any commission more terrible for a man than to have to announce the defeat of his own nation? to preach submission to the conqueror? to make himself disgraced as a traitor to his country?[2]

For Jeremiah this was not the point; God had given his verdict; the only repentance possible consists in the acceptance of this sentence. And in this act of acceptance lies their salvation. He knows, with the certitude which only a prophet can possess, that Babylon is the scourge of the Lord, meant to beat the nations as the corn is beaten upon the threshing floor—in order to sift the grain and disengage it from the straw. Against this tribunal, before which all nations will have to appear, no one can do anything. The cup of judgment is poured out: it must be drunk.[3]

But when everyone in the besieged city had lost heart, it was the prophet who bought a field, a sign of his certainty of future deliverance.[4]

Thus the prophet always looks like a man who does everything at the wrong time: he is a prophet of unhappiness in the midst of security; he denounces the false peace

---

[1] Jer. 34 (Moffatt Version); cf. Ex. 21.1-2; Deut. 15.12-18.
[2] See especially Jer. 37; 38.
[3] Jer. 25.15-33.　　　　[4] Jer. 32.6-15.

which is really only slavery;[1] he is the prophet of deliverance and of pardon at the height of the storm of disaster.[2]

For his views are the views of God, not of men. His gaze pierces the crust of appearances, and discovers the hidden meaning of history, of this history which God is writing with, and in spite of, men, whose final word will be resurrection and deliverance. He weighs men and events with something of the freedom of God himself. But to the extent in which God speaks through his mouth, he bleeds—with a sorrow which is both human and divine.

This was Jeremiah, the Prophet of the nations.

7

THE RETURN TO THE PROMISED LAND

Read Isaiah : chapters 40; 45; 52.13-53.12; 60

THE CAPTIVITY IN Babylon was not only exile—in itself a very hard experience. The Chosen People had been stripped of all that constituted the very reason of their existence : all the visible signs of the promises and fidelity of God—the Promised Land, the Holy City, the House of David, and above all, the Temple, where this Chosen People came to worship, to offer sacrifice, and to receive the divine forgiveness.

The distress of the exiles is expressed in Psalm 137 :

'By the rivers of Babylon
There we sat down, yea, we wept,
When we remembered Zion.
Upon the willows in the midst thereof

[1] Jer. 6.13-14.   [2] Jer. 31.1-6.

We hanged up our harps,
For there they that led us captive required of us songs,
And they that wasted us required of us mirth, saying,
"Sing us one of the songs of Zion."
How shall we sing the Lord's song
In a strange land?
If I forget thee, O Jerusalem,
Let my right hand forget her cunning.'

The Book of Lamentations is one long dirge over the abandoned city: 'Has God cast off his people for ever?'

And now, behold, God intervenes. By the hands of a heathen, Cyrus, he gives liberty to the captives. The song of sorrow is followed by the song of gratitude and joy:

'When the Lord turned again the captivity of Zion
We were like unto them that dream.
Then was our mouth filled with laughter,
And our tongue with singing. . . .
They that sow in tears shall reap in joy.
Though he goeth on his way weeping,
bearing forth the seed:
He shall come again with joy,
Bringing his sheaves with him' (Ps. 126).

An edict of Cyrus, King of Persia, has permitted the Israelites to return home. In so doing he is an instrument of God.[1] Israel knows that she owes her liberation to God alone. And this liberation is a grace, because it is a sign of God's pardon:

'Comfort ye, comfort ye, my people, saith your God.
Speak ye comfortably to Jerusalem, and cry unto her
That her warfare is accomplished, that her iniquity
is pardoned; that she hath received of the Lord's hand
double for all her sins.'[2]

This forgiveness is true liberation.
The restoration was certainly not the triumphant return

[1] Isa. 45.   [2] Isa. 40.1-2.

of which the captives had dreamed. Jerusalem was destroyed, the country had been devastated. The Bible contains an echo of this miserable situation :

'Ye have sown much and bring in little;
Ye eat, but ye have not enough;
Ye drink, but ye are not filled with drink;
Ye clothe you, but there is none warm;
And he that earneth wages earneth wages to put it
into a bag with holes' (Hag. 1.6).

The aftermath of war is hard, and selfishness reappears. The Temple was only rebuilt twenty years after the first Return; at first, no one thought of anything but his own house.[1] Many of the Jews remained behind and settled in Babylon : life there was easier than in a country which had been devastated by war. And among those who did return how many had truly turned to God? This new liberation was only an outward sign of a much deeper liberation which was still to come.

Nevertheless, this material liberation had a value of its own. Once more God gave his People space where they could live in accordance with their faith and their traditions; weakened, but also purified by trial, Israel was still the bearer of the promises of her Lord—until he come; and this time of waiting was to last for more than five hundred years.

Never again, it is true, will Israel achieve true political independence, save for the period of the Maccabean revolt. But she was able to keep her laws, her language, her customs, a certain administrative autonomy, and her own ways of worship.

The book of Nehemiah has a moving chapter in Israel's history on the rebuilding of the walls of Jerusalem : it pictures a whole people holding in one hand the trowel, and in the other the sword, united in one faith and one will.[2] The story of Nehemiah also reminds us that there is no

---

[1] Hag. 1 and 2.   [2] Neh. 1-6 (incl.); 12.27-43.

liberty without justice.[1] He reminds us finally that the foundation of the life of this nation, and of its liberties, is faith in the living God; it is the renewal of the Covenant.[2]

But how far all this is from the Age of Gold of which men have dreamed!

Among the believers there were those who had understood that God alone can build the city of justice and peace which he has promised to his own. A Messiah will come, the true Anointed of the Lord, and he will create this new Jerusalem which men cannot build.

The chapters 40-66 of Isaiah announce this coming. They set before our eyes the figure of the Liberator: at first it is Cyrus. But then another figure appears: it is not that of a powerful king such as Israel had expected, but that of the *Servant*, who will 'not lift up his voice', who will not 'cry aloud in the streets', who will not 'break the broken reed' but who proclaims justice with truth. He will be the 'light of the nations', he will open the eyes of the blind, he will set the captives free.[3] Further, he will take upon his own shoulders the sicknesses and the sins of his people. He will be rejected and despised of men, but a day will come when the kings of the earth will fall down and worship him.[4]

Then the New Jerusalem will see the glory of God rising upon her. She will attract all the nations. There will be no more devastation, no more ruins. She will know *salvation*.[5]

The prophets of Israel do not describe an abstract heaven, but a 'new creation', in which liberty and joy will reign; where each man will enjoy the vine he has planted, the house which he has built, where no one will work in vain, where peace will reign; where the wolf will lie down with the lamb.[6]

This is the final liberation: that in which God will take away the sin of the world, where his justice and his love will shine upon a world reconciled with its Creator.[7]

[1] Neh. 5.
[2] Neh. 8 and 9.
[3] Isa. 42.1-7; cf. 49.1-7.
[4] Isa. 52.13 to 53.12.
[5] Isa. 60.
[6] Isa. 65.17-25.
[7] Isa. 11.1-9.

The Old Testament is an incomplete book; it ends with a great hope which has not yet been fufilled. Someone has to come to proclaim liberty to the nations.

8

QUESTIONS OF A BELIEVER

IN THIS CHAPTER we are going to speak of the *liberty of the believer in the presence of God.*

This liberty, which we have already observed in Jeremiah, breaks out in the Book of Psalms and in the Book of Job. It is the exact opposite of the resignation of the Stoic or the fatalist. God is living, he can act, and the believer, with an amazing liberty, asks him why he is silent and apparently doing nothing.

1. *The 'Why' of the Psalmist.* Read Psalms 32; 10; 42; 43

The Book of Psalms is the hymn-book of Israel; but what a force there is in these songs! What a sincerity! These men do not make themselves out to be more religious or more humble than they are. If a man has a good conscience he says so; by this he does not mean that he is perfect, but simply that he has put his trust in God and has obeyed him. Then why does God not protect him better against his enemies?

Another, who has done wrong, confesses his sin; and having done so he feels that he has been released from a great weight. He sings of his liberation, of this wonder of grace and pardon entering into his life, removing this heavy burden caused by unconfessed sin. (See Ps. 32.)

Every believer who looks at the world, and what is going on in it, asks himself questions: why is there so much injustice? why does evil so often triumph? Such questions are often regarded as a sign of unbelief; they may be; but they can also be a sign of the sincerity of the believer, of his seriousness. The Psalmist does not put his question to men, but to God himself; that is perhaps the point which marks the difference between unbelief and faith. And behold, God answers : not necessarily at once. . . . It may be that he is silent for a long time. But he does reply. And we see the soul of the Psalmist reassured as he sings of his certainty and his peace. This does not always mean that the enemy has disappeared. But God is there. Listen to Ps. 10 :

'Why standest thou afar off, O Lord?
Why hidest thou thyself in times of trouble?
In the pride of the wicked the poor is hotly pursued . . .

All his thoughts are, There is no God . . .
He saith in his heart, God hath forgotten :
He hideth his face; he will never see it . . .'

Thus the wicked man triumphs. And the believer cries out :

'Arise, O Lord! O God, lift up thine hand :
Forget not the poor!
Wherefore doth the wicked contemn God?
And say in his heart, Thou wilt not require it?'[1]

It is the honour of God which is at stake when he allows his own people to be crushed! But now see how the tone changes :

'Thou hast seen it; for thou beholdest mischief and
    spite,
To take it into thy hand;
The helpless committeth himself unto thee;
Thou hast been the helper of the fatherless (10.14).

Once more the shadows are lifted by the light which comes from a presence which enables us to endure everything.

[1] Ps. 10 (RV).

We find the same spirit in Pss. 42-3 (which are really only one psalm). This is the mournful chant of the exile who languishes far from the Temple where he used to worship God. He is athirst for God, as a hart pants for running water . . . he thirsts to see the Face of God.

Around him are the people who mock him, saying 'Where is thy God?'

And three times he meets the temptation to despair by an act of faith :

> 'Why art thou cast down, O my soul?
> And why art thou disquieted within me?
> Hope thou in God :
> For I shall yet praise him
> For the health of his countenance.'

Does not the unique liberty of the people of God in exile consist in the fact that everything may be taken from them *except their faith*? Further: in the solitude and deprivations of the exile the faithful in Israel rediscovered contact with the living God. This fidelity alone kept them alive.

Several Psalms are songs of deliverance. Sometimes a cry of gratitude from a sick man whom God has saved from death, or of a man who has been falsely accused and whose innocence has been proved, or of a sinner whose sin is forgiven. These are all concrete deliverances, actual life-experiences :

> 'I love the Lord, because he hath heard
> My voice and my supplications.
> Because he hath inclined his ear unto me,
> Therefore will I call upon him as long as I live.
> The cords of death compassed me.
> And the pains of Sheol gat hold upon me :
> I found trouble and sorrow.
> Then called I upon the name of the Lord,
> O Lord, I beseech thee, deliver my soul' (Ps. 116).

I will take the cup of salvation
And call upon the name of the Lord . . .

    .   .   .   .   .

'I shall not die, but live,
And declare the works of the Lord.
The Lord hath chastened me sore,
But he hath not given me over unto death'
    (Ps. 118.17-18).

Thus, always afresh, God appears as the *Liberator:* he who breaks the chains of the slave, the chains of sickness and of death; and also those hidden chains which bind a man to his past sins.

Already with these Psalms we are on the threshold of the Gospel of the Word made flesh, of our flesh, in order to make us free with his freedom.

2. *The Rebellion of Job.* Read especially chapters 1 to 3 (inclusive) and 13; 19; 38 and 42

This Book of Job is extraordinary. It is very long and we will not try to analyse it. But what matters is to understand why Job, in all his rebellion, was nearer to God than his friends with their piety.

Job suffers from a whole series of catastrophes; he loses all his property, all his children; and he submits to the will of God. Then he has a terrible disease which devours his body, and his flesh becomes corrupt before his eyes.

Then his friends come upon the scene; at first they are silent, which is wise. But Job breaks out:

    'Let the day perish in which I was born.

    .   .   .   .   .

    Why died I not from the womb?'

Immediately his pious friends are shocked; they bring into the discussion a whole arsenal of theological arguments: if Job is suffering it must be due to his sin, so he ought to admit his guilt and accept his punishment.

Job says NO—he has no sense of having offended against

God; wearied by the arguments of his friends he calls upon God himself, with all the vehemence and frankness of an honest man. He pours out everything that is in his heart to God—his revolt, and his waiting, his despair, and his faith.

Then God intervenes in the debate; he treats Job as a man, as a person who confronts him, and must be treated seriously :

> 'Gird up now thy loins like a man;
> For I will demand of thee, and declare thou unto me,
> Where wast thou when I laid the foundations of the earth?'[1]

It is the Almighty who is speaking, the Creator of heaven and earth and before this divine revelation Job becomes humble and meek :

> 'I had heard of thee by the hearing of the ear;
> But now mine eye seeth thee.
> Wherefore I abhor myself,
> and repent in dust and ashes.'[2]

Job knows no more than before of the causes of his suffering. But he has come into contact with God : and his soul lives.

And then God expresses his anger with Job's friends, because—he says to them—'ye have not spoken of the thing that is right, as my servant Job hath'.

What does this mean? Job, tortured upon his dungheap, speaks to God with the freedom of a free man; he believes in God; he loves God; but he does not understand the suffering which crushes him, and he cries out in his suffering without trying to hide his doubts or his despair; he is completely honest.

His friends only offer him pious platitudes; they do not really enter into his suffering; they set themselves up to judge him; their sermons sound hollow.

[1] Job 38.3-4.   [2] Job 42.5-6.

Job speaks openly before God and before men; it is the only liberty which he retains. But it is this honesty, even in revolt, which makes him a true man.

There are revolts which are more truly acts of faith than many an act of pious resignation.

3. Conclusion

These few chapters from the Old Testament which we have been studying show us two things.

First, a humanity which by its break with its Creator has placed itself entirely under the sign of sin and death. 'In thy sight shall no man living be justified' exclaims the psalmist.[1]

Secondly, we have seen that where God speaks to a man and he listens, this word makes him amazingly free, with regard to men and events. He becomes a 'sign' of that liberation which God promises to those who belong to him. In the same way, when God delivers his people from the slavery of Egypt, or from the Babylonian captivity, he makes this people a 'sign' of the coming deliverance.

But these are still only signs and promises. Humanity still remains enslaved by the evil forces which tear it to pieces; it remains the prisoner of death.

To break these bonds another must come. He has come: that is the good news of the New Testament.

[1] Ps. 143.2; 14.3; cf. Job 4.17; 9.2; 25.4.

PART TWO

THE LIBERATOR

THE GOSPEL IS good news: the good news of the victory of Jesus Christ over sin and death.

God himself has come down to earth in the person of his Son. He has identified himself wholly with our humanity; he has borne the burden of our sins upon the Cross. He has confronted and overcome the adversary who holds humanity captive. 'God was in Christ reconciling the world unto himself.'[1]

This is the great mystery of the Gospel, and it is a mystery of love. God wants to make us his children. He wants us to give ourselves to him of our own free will, in gratitude and love. In order to accomplish this purpose he pays a great price: the Cross on which his beloved Son, his sinless Son, dies. And this Son gives his life freely. Through the whole of his ministry, in his obedience unto death, he reveals to us what it means to love God, and to love his brethren.

In this total gift of himself, in his holiness, in his love, he is this 'image' of God which constitutes our vocation as men.

He calls us to believe this, to follow him, in order that he may recreate this 'image'—within us—and he alone can do this—he wants to make us *free men*—free with his freedom.

Jesus enters history as the only free man who has ever lived upon earth. The philosopher Epictetus complained that he had never met such a man. This is the messenger whom the Old Testament foretold, and for whom Israel waited, and lo! he has come; he really lived, for thirty

[1] II Cor. 5.19.

years, in this corner of Palestine; he used to walk by the Lake of Galilee.

We must contemplate Jesus in all his movements and his gestures, in every word he spoke, in every one of his acts, in order to grasp this mystery of freedom which is in him; we must join the crowd which surrounds him and let his gaze pierce our hearts to the very bottom—to our heart's deepest secrets: this gaze which sees, which knows, which judges and which sets us free.

9

THE ADVERSARY

Read Matthew 4.1-11; Mark 8.11-13, 27-33

JESUS WAS BORN in an occupied country. Palestine was part of the Roman Empire. At the moment when Jesus was born, it was governed by the king Herod the Great—detested by his subjects who looked upon him as a usurper. Jesus began his ministry in a divided Palestine; another Herod governed Galilee, while a Roman official, Pilate, was Procurator of Judaea.

Politics was a burning question; one rebellion followed another; there were the extreme nationalists, the 'Zealots'; there were the pious Jews who were looking for the new David, the Messiah,[1] and were counting on him to deliver Israel from the yoke of Rome.

Here is the great deliverance foretold by the Prophets. We do not really understand the story of the temptation

---

[1] *Messiah*—'Anointed'—In Israel (in early times) high priests and kings were anointed with oil, as a sign that God had chosen them for their respective office—'Christ' is the English form of the Greek word for 'anointed'.

of Jesus unless we remember this atmosphere of political tension, hope, and expectation. The crowds—and even the disciples—hoped to the end that Jesus would be the political Messiah who would set Israel free from the foreign yoke,[1] and from misery, hunger, and oppression. Was not this a legitimate expectation? Had not the Prophets promised all this?

Among the Jews at this time there were others who were not looking for a temporal king, but for the Son of man who was to come upon the clouds of heaven. He would manifest himself by 'signs', by astonishing miracles.[2] His coming would mean the end of the world, and the coming of the New Age, when Jerusalem would become the capital city for the whole world of nations.

The Old Testament, as we have seen, also gives us a third vision of things to come, that of the Servant who was rejected, misunderstood, who bears the sins of his people. He will be elevated to the Throne; but his way passes through death.[3]

Jesus was nourished on the Scriptures. He knew what his people were expecting; he understood their expectations and their suffering. But he knew too that for him the only way willed by God was the way of the Servant: his way must be that of obedience; it will pass through death. For he cannot defeat Satan with his own weapons; he can only defeat him by fulfilling all the righteousness of God, by incarnating his love. It is to the humble, not to the strong and powerful of this world that the kingdom is promised.[4]

It is as he lives his human life in obedience to God, without any other weapon than that of faith, that Jesus will conquer the enemy, submit to his final attacks, and open up, to all those who believe in him, the way of liberation.

In allowing himself to be baptized by John the Baptist Jesus proclaimed his solidarity with his guilty people: he repented *with* and *for* his people, although *he* had no need

---

[1] John 6.15.
[2] Dan. 7.13-14; Mark 8.11-13.
[3] Isa. 53.
[4] Luke 1.52.

of repentance. It was by thus humiliating himself, by identification in love, that he revealed himself as the Son of his Father—the well-beloved Son.[1] From this moment he took upon himself the burden of the sin of his people, which he was to carry to the end.

It was then that the Holy Spirit led him into the wilderness, in order that he should be 'tempted of the devil'. What does this temptation mean? It is the whole work of Jesus as Messiah which is at stake.

The temptation in the wilderness is the solitary conflict which precedes his public ministry. It concerns the *methods* of this ministry.

One day he would express this very plainly: 'No one can enter into the house of the strong man, and spoil his goods, except he first bind the strong man, and then he will spoil his house.'[2]

Jesus could only liberate those who were bound by Satan because he himself was free from his domination, because he had unmasked and defeated him.

We should note that it is the Holy Spirit who leads Jesus into the wilderness. God is with him in the conflict. Later on, Jesus will warn his disciples that they are to fear the tempter, and to pray that God will not allow them to be exposed to his assaults.[3] For the enemy is very strong.

In order to understand the meaning of this narrative as fully as possible we should remember the first couple of human beings. The tempting voice of the Serpent showed Eve some beautiful fruit: 'If you eat this you will be like a god! You will be your own master! You will be free . . .' Since then the whole human race has been eating this fruit, which was supposed to make them 'free', and they taste the bitter results.

This time it is the Son of God whom Satan is addressing: he is far more prudent now; he waits till Jesus is exhausted by fasting. This is the best moment to attack, with a proposition which sounds very innocent: 'If thou art the Son

---

[1] Matt. 3.13-17.   [2] Mark 3.27.   [3] Luke 22.31; cf. Matt. 6.13.

C

of God, command that these stones become bread.' In other
words: 'If you are the Son of God—Are you not at home
here? Act as if you were! You are master here.' Here it is
not a question of making oneself equal to God, as in the
case of Adam and Eve; the devil is merely suggesting that
Jesus should exercise his legitimate powers. Jesus at once
exposes the trap: 'Man shall not live by bread alone but
by every word that proceedeth out of the mouth of God.'

Where Satan says 'Thou', Jesus replies: 'God.' The life
of the Son of man upon earth will be one of obedience and
humiliation: 'The foxes have holes, and the birds of the
heaven have nests; but the Son of man hath not where to
lay his head' (RV Luke 9.58). Upon this earth he has all the
rights of his Father. But he will not use any of them in
order to save himself. The crowds round the Cross cried
out in mockery: 'He hath saved others; himself he cannot
save.' It was true: in order to save others he accepted hunger, poverty, death. He willed to descend to the depths of
our misery as man, and to make it his own—he only de-
sired one thing: the will of God, and his Word.

Then Satan tried a second line of attack; Israel was expecting a Messiah who would come down from heaven,
and would impress himself upon everyone by signs and
wonders. Why not fufil this expectation? Show that you
are really the One whom God has sent.

Jesus answers: 'To do this would be to tempt God.'

We note here that Satan uses a verse of Scripture to
tempt Jesus;[1] and Jesus answers him with another verse of
Scripture. The letter of Scripture can be an instrument of
Satan—the Spirit of God alone can open up to us its true
meaning. We note also that Jesus does not expect God to
protect him from suffering. In choosing the way of obedience he is also choosing the way of the Cross.

Then, as a last attempt, Satan shows his true colours. He
shows Jesus all the powers of the earth, 'the kingdoms of
this world, and the glory of them'—and says: 'Do you not

---

[1] Matt. 4.5-7.

know that all this belongs to ME, Satan, and that I alone can give it to you?'

Was Satan wholly wrong? One day Jesus was to declare that his 'Kingdom was not of this world'. He himself will call Satan the 'Prince of this world'. He admits the strength of the occupying power. The reign of God which Jesus proclaims and incarnates is precisely a *new* world; a world which will break the other in pieces. Ah! truly the days of Satan are numbered . . . But at the moment he is in command! And he will bring up all the forces *of this world* against Jesus.

Do we not often feel this power of Satan? Human affairs bear his imprint; in order to 'succeed' in life, how many concessions we have to make.

And the Jews of the time of Jesus were expecting a Messiah who would *succeed upon the earth*; who would drive out the Romans by rebellion—and if need be by a reign of terror. Afterwards would come the reign of justice and peace.

Jesus grew up in a nation full of this expectation. Before his coming how many men had come who were regarded as messengers of God, who preached a Holy War!

Thus, at this critical moment, he knew that he had to reject even the legitimate hopes of his oppressed people. He would not be a Zealot.

For him the end did not justify the means. He rejected the great Messianic dream of temporal victory. When his 'hour' came he would not ask for a 'legion of angels' to protect him. He would allow himself to be led out to die.

Satan withdrew. He was waiting for 'another occasion'.[1] He will be there, watching, when the crowds want to make Jesus King.[2] He will return in the guise of a disciple, of a friend, who had just confessed his faith, and the moment afterwards was indignant and protested against the idea that Jesus could suffer and die : 'God forbid that this should ever happen to *you*.' We feel the force of the attack in the

Luke 4.13.   [2] John 6.15.

severity with which Jesus repelled Peter's protest : 'Get thee behind me, Satan! thou art a stumbling-block unto me : for thou mindest not the things of God, but the things of men.'[1] Once for all Jesus had unmasked the adversary. And that enabled him to recognize him under all the fresh disguises that Satan assumed—even the mask of a disciple and a friend. The Epistle to the Hebrews says that Jesus was 'tempted in all points like as we are, yet without sin'.[2] That is what makes him able to set us free.

The decisive victory will be won upon the Cross, and its final manifestation will not appear to all eyes until the end of the world. But every person liberated in his body and in his soul is a sign of this victory. Hearing of the deliverances worked by his first disciples Jesus already saw 'Satan fallen as lightning from heaven'.[3]

10

BROKEN CHAINS—1

CONQUEROR OF DEMONS

Read Mark 1.21-28; 2.1-12; 5.1-20

AFTER HAVING MET and conquered the enemy in the solitude of the desert, Jesus begins his ministry in the power of the Spirit.[4]

The Gospel of Mark shows him to us from the very first moment in conflict with the demons. They were the first to recognize in him the 'holy One of God', and they were afraid of him.

[1] Matt. 16.21-23 (RV).   [2] Heb. 4.15-16 (RV).
[3] Luke 10.18.   [4] Luke 4.13-14.

The sick man possessed by a demon identified himself with the evil power which possessed him: 'What have we to do with thee, thou Jesus of Nazareth? art thou come to destroy us? . . .'[1] Nothing was more true: Jesus *had* come into the world in order to conquer the demons, to break the chains forged by the demons. He has all power, because Satan has no power over him.

Jesus knew that the power of these evil forces was terribly real. He saw them at work. He knew the demons, and the demons knew him.

But some modern people will say: 'do you really believe in the existence of demons?' To this question I would reply, first of all: Jesus believed this. When he speaks of them it is not a figure of speech. He was aware that there are evil forces in this world which are very active, and that these forces have a leader, whose whole effort is concentrated on the destruction of the work of God: to sow division, while it is the work of God to create unity, the fruit of love. Satan is the great divider.

The spirit which agitated the Gadarene demoniac declared that his name was 'legion'.[2] The Roman legions were well organized armies; evil too is well organized. It divides man against himself, and this sense of being 'multiple' may even lead to insanity; but which of us does not know the feeling of having several persons in oneself: 'For that which I do I know not; for not what I would, that do I practise; but what I hate, that I do,' says St Paul.[3]

The sick people whom Jesus cured knew that they were possessed by an evil spirit which they could not possibly drive out. Such cases of 'possession' still exist today, and sorcery and magic play a dangerous game with these evil forces. The distinctive element in these forces is that they actually end in 'possessing' a person utterly. Where the fear of the spirits has disappeared they take other forms: they possess a person by drink, by gambling, by the senses, by the love of money, or by an overweening pride; and

[1] Mark 1.24; cf. 3.11-12; 5.7.　　[2] Mark 5.9.　　[3] Rom. 7.15.

such a person becomes their 'thing', a slave of his passion.

People will say that these forms of 'possession' are quite different from demon possession. Perhaps . . . but I am not so sure. What *is* sure is that it is in the power of God, and in his hands alone, to break the power of *all* these forms of slavery.

And it is this Almighty power of God which Jesus came to proclaim, in all his words and acts: 'And they were all amazed, insomuch that they questioned among themselves, saying, What is this? a new teaching? with authority he commandeth even the unclean spirits and they obey him.'[1]

In Jesus, as in God, every word is an *act*. 'For he spake and it was done.'[2]

Jesus commands, and the sick man goes away healed and pardoned. For healing and forgiveness are two aspects of the same reality. Sin entering into the world has laid its mark upon both bodies and souls. Jesus has come to save the whole man; to give him back his health. Thus every act of healing and of forgiveness is a sign of the coming Kingdom; this Kingdom, in the person of Jesus, is already present.

To the seventy disciples whom Jesus sent out on a mission he says: 'Heal the sick that are therein, and say unto them, the Kingdom of God is come nigh unto you.'[3]

The Gospel tells the story of a paralytic whom his friends carry to Jesus:[4] Nothing stops them: the crowds block the entrance, so they go up the outside stair to the roof—the terrace of the house—and after they have cleared a space they let down the stretcher into the place where Jesus was standing. Jesus, seeing the faith of these men, says to the paralytic: 'Son! thy sins are forgiven thee.' Was that what the disabled man was expecting? . . . did he know, deep down in his heart, that he was paying for the sins of the past? Did Jesus see in his eyes a look of anguish which spoke of a deeper suffering than that due to his malady? In the eyes of Jesus, at any rate, it was *this word* which was

[1] Mark 1.27.   [2] Ps. 33.9.   [3] Luke 10.9.   [4] Mark 2.1-12.

the most important. He had come to set men free, and he
alone has the power to set them free. The bystanders were
beginning to mutter : 'By what right? . . .' Then Jesus spoke
another royal word : 'I say unto thee, arise, take up thy
bed, and go unto thy house.' And lo, we see a man set free
from the whole of his past life. Before him there opens up
the vista of a completely new life.

Does this mean that there is a direct connection between
sin and disease? Sometimes this is the case; we pay for some
excesses in our body as well as in our soul. But Jesus for-
bids us to establish such a relation too swiftly. When he
was confronted by the man born blind, his disciples asked
him : 'Lord, who did sin? this man or his parents?' he rejected the question, saying : 'Neither did this man sin, nor
his parents; but that the works of God should be made
manifest in him.'[1]

We are often only too ready to judge others, to see their
responsibility in what happens to them. Jesus is never tired
of reminding us that he came not to condemn but to save.
All human misery may become, by faith, a means of glori-
fying God.

Jesus came to proclaim liberty to the captives. Healing
and salvation are two sides of this liberation. The healing
of the body is only one 'sign', among others, of a deeper
healing that goes down to the roots of our being. Jesus does
not wish us to seek it for itself alone.

He could have had an easy popularity as a healer; but he
distrusted this for fear it should obscure the true purpose
of his mission. The Gospel shows him to us fleeing from
the crowds and retiring into solitude. And when his disciples, excited by his success, came to him saying, 'All are
seeking thee,' he answered : 'Let us go elsewhere into the
next towns, that I may preach there also; for therefore came
I forth.'[2]

The preaching of the good news comes first. God has
come down to men, that is the great message. Every con-

[1] John 9.1-5.   [2] Mark 1.32-38.

crete deliverance is a sign of this coming and ought to be
received as such.

The decisive sign will be the Resurrection of Jesus from
the dead. In liberating souls and bodies in the course of his
ministry on earth, Jesus was proclaiming that final liberation when the Prince of Life will put Satan under his feet,
Satan the Prince of Death.[1]

II

BROKEN CHAINS—2

1. *The Demon of Money*

Read Matt. 6.23-34; Luke 6.24-26; 12.13-34; 16.19-31;
Mark 10.17-31

AMONG THE DEMONS he had come to fight, Jesus gave
a very special place to 'Mammon'. Now, mammon means
riches: it is the god of money.

'No man can serve two masters: for either he will hate
the one and serve the other; or else he will hold to the one
and despise the other. Ye cannot serve God and mammon.'[2]

Is it really mammon which is the rival of God in our
hearts? Do the cares connected with money take an in-
creasing place in our daily life, and indeed take up more
room than our concern for the Kingdom of God? At bottom this is the heart of the question.

For himself, Jesus chose the liberty of the poor man, that
is to say, the liberty of one whose treasure is in heaven
and has nothing upon earth that needs protection: 'For
where thy treasure is, there will thy heart be also.'[3] It is

[1] Acts 2.24; 3.15; cf. I Cor. 15.26.   [2] Matt. 6.24.   [3] Matt. 6.19-21.

not that he thinks there is any special *virtue* in poverty.
But if a person's whole concern is for the Kingdom of God,
he will not want to be encumbered with the affairs of this
world; he can commit his need for daily bread to the Lord
who employs him. Jesus wanted his disciples to be entirely
given to God, and therefore as free from care as the birds
of the air; not improvident, but free from anxiety.[1]

Jesus returned to this subject of riches so often because
he saw men wasting their time, their strength, and perhaps
even their souls for something which tomorrow would be
taken from them. He wanted them to realize that such behaviour was extremely foolish—'Thou foolish one . . . this
night is thy soul required of thee!'[2]

In all this Jesus seems to have started from a very concrete experience : there were not many rich and powerful
people among those who followed him to the Mountain of
the Beatitudes, and whom he called 'happy'.[3] Among those
whom he invited to the great feast of the Kingdom there
were many people who were 'too busy' to come. One had
just bought a piece of land : ought he not to go and inspect
it? Another had just bought 'five yoke of oxen'. Another
had just married a wife . . . How could such people, in the
midst of such urgent and important matters, find time for
God?[4]

There was nothing of the demagogue in Jesus. He did not
hate riches because he was poor. He knew that the poor
man's envy of the rich and his 'anxiety' could be just as
destructive of liberty as the possessions of the rich man.
For it is possible to have one's mind full to the brim with the
desire for 'possessions', just as we can have our minds full
of the things which we do possess. In both instances it is
'money' which 'holds' us. The well-known story of the rich
young man shows us a man of whom it was said that
Jesus looked at him and 'loved' him; this was a man who
was drawn to Jesus but who, at the last moment, drew

[1] Matt. 6.24-31; cf. Luke 12.22-31.   [2] Luke 12.17-21.
[3] Luke 6.20-26.   [4] Luke 14.15-24.

back and went sadly away, 'for he had great possessions'.[1]

Jesus wants us to be free for God. And his call to 'leave all' is accompanied by a promise: to those who *seek first his Kingdom*, the rest will be added.[2] To those who have left all for him he promises that they will receive a hundredfold: houses, brothers, sisters, mothers, children . . .[3]

What does this mean? It means that those who really give their lives to God make two wonderful discoveries: first, that they really have a *Father* in heaven; a Father who looks after them, in good days and in bad, with infinite kindness and care, a Father who never forsakes them. 'The very hairs of your head are all numbered', says Jesus: God knows you. God knows what you need. He also knows the limits of your powers. He is watching over you. There is nothing to be afraid of, nothing at all.

The second discovery is this: that we enter into a new family, where sharing, mutual aid, is (or ought to be) the rule. One day, looking at his disciples, Jesus said: 'Behold my mother and my brethren! For whosoever shall do the will of God, the same is my brother, and sister, and mother.'[4]

This family is the community which he came to create, and in the Acts of the Apostles we see to how great a degree the first Christians felt their solidarity with each other. Wherever the Church is alive, there this miracle of which Jesus speaks takes place: God gives us back a hundredfold that which we have given to him.

Here however we must guard against a misunderstanding. Jesus does not promise us an *easy* life, but a life which is blessed by God; which is quite different. How could One who had chosen for himself a life of privation and conflict promise a limited, sheltered, life to his disciples? Our text speaks of 'houses' and 'fields', but also of 'persecutions'. The apostle Paul tells us that he has known 'labour and travail, hunger and thirst, cold and nakedness'.[5] He had to work

[1] Mark 10.17-27.   [2] Luke 12.32-34.   [3] Mark 10.28-31.
[4] Mark 3.31-35.   [5] II Cor. 11.27.

with his hands to earn his bread. But he was able to exclaim: 'I know how to be abased, and I know also how to abound: in everything and in all things have I learned the secret to be filled and to be hungry, both to abound and to be in want. I can do all things in him that strengtheneth me.'[1]

It is *this liberty* that the Lord wants to give to his own disciples.

We are living in a time when perhaps more than in the time of Jesus material things tend to take the first place. When we speak of 'money' we mean comfort, and also prestige, influence: which of us does not feel a little desire for this? We ought to add that for many housewives anxiety about 'daily bread' is a very real thing.

In all this greed for riches the Christian can bear a real witness by his interior liberty which enables him to enjoy the good things of this world without clinging to them; he can leave the morrow to God, and (this is more difficult) he can also leave the future of his loved ones to God's care.

2. *The Demon of Fear*

Read Mark 4.35-41

Do you know this 'demon'? Has he not attacked you at some particular moment or another? Sometimes this demon assaults the bravest people: e.g. in a moment of great danger or when we are in great anxiety about someone we love. We are afraid of 'tomorrow'; afraid of poverty; afraid of sickness; afraid of old age; afraid of death. Some people have a fear of spirits.

The Gospel contains a magnificent story: a storm has burst upon the Lake of Galilee. The disciples were afraid. Jesus was in the stern of the boat asleep on the cushion. His disciples roused him, crying out: 'Master, don't you

[1] Phil. 4.12.

mind that we are on the point of drowning?' He ordered
the waves to abate, 'and the wind ceased and there was a
great calm'. Then he looked at them in astonishment, and
said: 'Why are ye fearful? Have ye not yet faith?'[1]

When fear seizes us we should let the words of Jesus
echo and re-echo in our ears: 'Why are you afraid?' We
must take refuge in his calmness. He is not only Master of
the Lake in the hour of storm; he is the Lord of history.
He is the Master of our life and of our death. He holds our
little life in his all-mighty hands. He has conquered death
for us.

'Who shall separate us from the love of Christ? Shall
tribulation, or anguish? or persecution? or famine, or
nakedness, or peril, or sword? . . . Nay, in all these things
we are more than conquerors through him that loved us.'[2]

Here we face the greatest mystery of all: in order to save
us from the anguish of death, he has tasted death for us
all, willingly. He drank this cup which the Father had given
him to the very dregs. And his cry of agony assures us that
he knows, that he understands, all our human fears, and
that he takes upon himself the terror of sin, the terror of
death, in order to deliver us from all fear.[3]

For though there are fears which are simply due to lack
of faith, there is a legitimate fear: that which makes a sinful man cry out in the presence of the Holy One like Isaiah:
'I am undone'[4] or like Peter: 'Depart from me, for I am a
sinful man, O Lord' 'for he was amazed, and all that were
with him, at the draught of the fishes which they had
taken.'[5]

The writer of the Apocalypse, seeing the Lord standing
before him in all his divine majesty, fell at his feet as one
dead. And the Risen Lord said to him: 'Fear not; I am the
first and the last, and the Living One; and I was dead, and
behold, I am alive for evermore, and I have the keys of
death and of Hades.'[6]

[1] Mark 4.35-41.   [2] Rom. 8.35-39.   [3] Mark 14.32-36; 15.33-37.
[4] Isa. 6.   [5] Luke 5.8.   [6] Rev. 1.17-18.

Henceforth the last enemy is under the feet of the conqueror.

The 'Fear Not' of Jesus includes the *whole of our life and
the whole of our death.*

12

THE LIBERTY OF JESUS IN HIS
CONTACT WITH PERSONS

Read Mark 2.13; 3.7; Luke 7.36-50; 19.1-10

WE ARE OFTEN tempted to judge people by their quali-
ties or their defects, by their social importance, or by the
services which they can render to us—or again in the light
of their ideas, or the ideas of the party or group to which
they happen to belong. There are the people whom we meet
'socially', and others with whom we do not mix. There are
people whom we regard as 'interesting', and others who are
'boring'; there are people whom it is 'useful' to know, and
whom we desire to please, and others from whom we do not
expect to get anything, and whom we tacitly 'forget' . . .

When we read the Gospels we see that Jesus judges people
from a totally different point of view. For him every human
being is a child of God, whom he wants to bring home to
the Father's house. He sees a sick world, waiting to be
healed, a world in chains, waiting to be set free. Hence for
him, people fall into two categories only : those who *know*
that they are sick and accept the great physician, and those
who don't want to admit that there is anything the matter
with them. He can do everything for the former; for the
latter he can do nothing; for what can a doctor do for someone who does not want to have anything to do with him?[1]

[1] Mark 2.15-17.

The problem for Jesus, so far as the Pharisees were concerned, was that these men were quite 'satisfied' with themselves. They had no sense of need.

The Pharisees were not wicked men; on the contrary, they were very religious people. The word 'Pharisee' means one who is 'separated' : they had separated from others in order that they might obey the law more fully; they took a great deal of trouble to keep the Sabbath very strictly. They gave bad company a wide berth. After making so many sacrifices they thought that they must be right with God.[1]

For people whose behaviour was so 'correct' the conduct of Jesus was embarrassing. In their eyes he did not keep the Sabbath as it should be kept, at least from the point of view of the Pharisees. Then he associated with people who were certainly 'outside the pale' of respectable society, and he even went to meals in their homes. And he was not in the least concerned about what people thought of him.[2]

The liberty of Jesus in his contact with persons was truly amazing : he invited himself to dinner with Levi the tax collector and with Zacchaeus the 'publican',[3] both of whom were minor officials in the pay of the occupying power, Rome; that is, with men whom every good Jew despised, as 'unclean'.

But he also called the 'Zealots' to follow him, that is to say, the ultra-Nationalists.[4] Then, one day, his disciples even found him calmly sitting on the parapet of a well and talking with a Samaritan woman; a woman! and a Samaritan at that! Even his disciples were astonished at such familiarity although they did not dare to say so![5]

Did not Jesus himself go so far as to tell the Pharisees that pagans will come from the East and from the West, and that even the publicans and the harlots would go into the King-

---

[1] There surely must have been some Pharisees whose hearts were open to the message of Jesus. At the same time, many of them were his most implacable enemies.
[2] Mark 2.23; 3.4.
[3] Luke 19.1-10.
[4] Luke 6.15.
[5] John 4.7-9; 27.

dom of God before them?[1] He gave the faith of a Roman officer as an example to the leading men of the synagogue (who were the 'pillars of the church' of that day!).

He was just as much at home at the table of the Pharisee as at that of Levi. He was always and everywhere perfectly himself. Only he was more merciful and gentle towards those whom the world despises and rejects, towards the 'lost sheep'. He was severe to those who had received a great deal from life and had not given any love in return. For Jesus, what counted was true repentance, the total gift of the heart. He was able to break the chains of a poor woman whom the world labelled as 'lost'; for him she was a human being, loved by God. In his whole attitude towards her he made her feel dignity as a woman : for the first time a man looked at her without lustful glances and without contempt; here, she began to realize, is 'someone who believes that even for *me* there is a possibility of a new and pure life'. Then her heart was full of gratitude and joy : 'Jesus believes that there is a future for me!' And she in her turn believed in him! and recognized in him One whom God had sent.

In order to understand this mystery of Jesus in his contact with persons, we should re-read the scene which took place in the house of Simon the Pharisee.[2] This man evidently thought he was conferring an honour on Jesus by inviting him—the poor itinerant preacher—to dinner. But he neglected to give him water to wash his feet, as Oriental hospitality required. And lo, in the midst of the meal a woman burst into the room. Jesus was reclining at table in the usual way. The woman stood behind him; she was in tears; she kissed his feet and anointed them with a precious perfume; then she dried them with her own hair. What a shocking scene! Simon was embarrassed, and even scandalized. He felt that Jesus ought to have known the kind of woman she was! (Who of us would not have been a little embarrassed if such a scene had taken place in our house?) But Jesus was not in the least embarrassed. He

[1] Matt. 8.11; 21.18-31.   [2] Luke 7.36-50.

knew very well the kind of woman she was : she was a child of the Kingdom, and the angels in heaven were singing for joy at her return![1]

He accepted the woman's gratitude in the way in which it was meant. His parable was a discreet warning to the Pharisee, who, never having realized the wonder of forgiveness, could not understand this outpouring of love.

In the time of Jesus woman was regarded by the Jews as an inferior being. Her husband could repudiate her. Jesus condemned this custom : he did not admit that the man has any more right than the woman to sever 'that which God hath joined together'.[2]

By his whole attitude towards women Jesus has wrought a silent revolution. Woman also has a soul! She also is a child of God and loved by him! We have just seen how he welcomed a poor woman belonging to those who were called 'lost'. There was also that other moving scene in which they brought to him a woman caught in the very act of adultery.[3] His enemies were watching him to see what he would do . . . and he simply said : 'He that is without sin among you, let him first cast a stone at her.' And these men, pierced in their consciences, 'went out one by one, beginning from the eldest, even unto the last'. And when they had all gone, Jesus looked at the woman and said very quietly : 'Neither do I condemn thee; go thy way; from henceforth sin no more.'

In the Gospel story we see women following Jesus, and helping him with their gifts.[4] The home at Bethany was one to which he loved to retire in the intimacy of friendship with the two sisters, Martha and Mary.[5] We see Mary anointing the Lord on the eve of his Passion; did she alone, among all his disciples, have a presentiment of the nearness of his death? . . . We see women at the foot of the Cross. And it was to them that it pleased the Lord to make known the first news of the Resurrection.[6] From that time forward

[1] Luke 15.7.   [2] Mark 10.1-12.   [3] John 8.1-11.
[4] Luke 8.2-3.   [5] Luke 10.38-42.   [6] Luke 24.1-12; cf. John 20.1-18.

woman was to have her place in the Church of Christ alongside of man, the recipient of the same grace, of the same salvation.[1]

We also see this perfect liberty of Jesus in respect of persons in his attitude towards the religious institutions of his day. He respected the Temple, but, recalling some words of Jeremiah, he accused the priests of having made it a 'den of robbers'[2]; he announced its destruction.

He respected the Law of Moses, or rather, he had come to *fulfil it* in obedience unto death; but he treated with the utmost severity those Pharisees who 'say and do not', and who add to the Law of God 'the traditions of men'.[3]

They closed the doors of the Kingdom to others, and did not go in themselves. For they neglected the greatest of all the Commandments: the love of God and of our neighbour. That is what Jesus calls to 'strain out the gnat and swallow the camel'.

Jesus always went behind the commandment to its intention. 'The Sabbath was made for man and not man for the Sabbath.' The rest of the seventh day was instituted by God in order that men might rejoice in him on that day; it was a symbol of the great repose of God, of the eternal Sabbath. To heal a human being on that day was precisely to proclaim the Reign of God, the great sabbath which was to come. When the Pharisees reproached Jesus for such acts of healing, it showed they were slaves to the 'letter' of the commandment. By their pettifogging rules they had killed love.[4]

This liberty of Jesus in dealing with human beings and with institutions is the very liberty of God himself, who looks at the heart, and not at outward appearances. It is the liberty of saving love which goes out towards human beings, where they are, to tell them that God loves them and is waiting for them.

[1] Gal. 3.27-28.   [2] Matt. 21.12-13.
[3] Matt. 23; Mark 7.   [4] Mark 2.23—3.6.

Human institutions, even ecclesiastical ones, are only instruments in the service of the great work of God which is the salvation of men.

13

THE TRUTH SHALL MAKE YOU FREE

Read John 8.24-45; chapter 9

IN HIS DISCOURSE to the Jews in Chapter 8 of the Gospel according to St John, Jesus explains clearly the meaning of his Mission : he has come to liberate the 'slaves', and to give them the status of 'sons'.

Immediately the Jews were indignant : 'We be Abraham's seed, and have never yet been in bondage to any man!' And Jesus replied : 'Everyone that committeth sin is the bond-servant of sin.'

Here Jesus put his finger on the real misery of our human condition : evil has entered so profoundly into us that it has become our master; it is no longer in our power to set ourselves free from it. It is true of course that we can resist certain particular temptations; but Jesus is thinking of those secret forms of 'slavery' which are so deep, and prevent us from loving God with a pure and total love, and our neighbour as ourselves.

If these Jews who were arguing against him really loved God, they would know that in his voice they were hearing the voice of his Son; but now they were rejecting him. Their father is 'the devil', the 'father of lies'. What a harsh judgment! it is a verdict which aims at unmasking the secret motive which is leading these men to refuse the offer of salvation. They believe that they are 'sons of Abraham', but they do not take seriously the promises which were made to him; they have neither his faith nor his obedience—they do not do his works. Because they have not really heard the word spoken to their ancestor, on whom they base their own position, their minds are closed to the Word of God, which is now being spoken to them, today, by Jesus.

How does one become a free man? Jesus says to those who 'have believed in him': 'If ye abide in my word, then are ye truly my disciples; and ye shall know the truth, and the truth shall make you free.'

To 'believe in him' is one thing; to 'abide' in his word is another: it means persevering in commitment to him, it is the obedience of every day. What matters is not merely to hear the word, but to put it into practice.[1] The word of Jesus is the rock on which our lives must be built. Then we shall be *truly* his disciples. We shall know 'the truth', and the truth will make us free.

What is this truth? Every word of God, every word of Jesus, is like a searchlight turned on to every corner of our life: we discover who God is and what we are. He comes to us with a promise, a judgment, a call. But the decisive word of God, the 'Word made flesh', is Jesus Christ himself. 'I am the Way, the Truth, and the Life.' It is in Jesus Christ that God has revealed to us all his holiness and all his mercy; 'He that hath seen me hath seen the Father.' It is also in Jesus Christ that we come to know ourselves. His dazzling light shows us our unfaithfulness. 'Depart from me, for I am a sinful man, O Lord!' This cry of Simon Peter becomes our own when we allow ourselves to be seen and judged by him. But because this searching gaze is that of the *Saviour*, the moment when he condemns us he raises us up, and we can only say with this same Simon: 'Lord, to whom shall we go? Thou hast the words of eternal life!'[2] or with Thomas: 'My Lord and my God.'[3]

'The Truth will make you free' . . . certainly we shall not become saints in a moment! all the fetters—whether evi-

[1] cf. Matt. 7.24-29.   [2] John 6.68.   [3] John 20.28.

dent or secret—of the 'Prince of this world' will not be broken at one fell swoop! the Christian life is *a growth into liberty*.

But our liberation consists in this: when Jesus Christ has laid his hand upon us, and we are living on his forgiveness, and we have committed our whole life to him, *we belong to him*: his word works in us, day after day, like a force of forgiveness and of life. Henceforward it is to him, the victor over the world, that we will look, and not to ourselves. He has made us 'sons' instead of 'slaves'.

What is characteristic of the true son? It is this: that he does not obey from constraint but from love. He enters wholly into the mind of his Father and makes that 'mind' his own. Jesus opens his heart to us as Son, when he tells us that it is his 'food' to do the will of God his Father,[1] when he tells us that the Son can do nothing of himself, he can only do what he sees the Father doing, 'for what things soever he doeth, these the Son also doeth in like manner'.[2]

To belong to God, is to be animated by his love;[3] it is to do his work.[4] Jesus lived this sonship in a unique and absolute sense; it is to this communion that he calls us; he wants to transform our hearts, so that the 'spirit of bondage' may disappear, and our hearts beat in union with his own. That is the final meaning of his coming into the world at all.

In order to effect this change, he has to strip us of our masks so that we may see, first of all, what we really are—what we are in the sight of God. The old self has to lay down its arms before the new one can be born. That is what Jesus calls the 'new birth'. All the wisdom of Nicodemus, a doctor of the law, is no good to him until he understands this.[5]

The turning-point in the conversation of Jesus with the Samaritan woman was reached when Jesus uncovered her past. She ran off to the village and said: 'Come, see a man

[1] John 4.34.   [2] John 5.19.   [3] John 5.42.
[4] John 9.4.   [5] John 3.1-8.

which told me all things that ever I did : can this be the Christ?' It was only the first step : she saw that she was *known* but already she had begun to discern that this man was 'more than a prophet'; already she was trying to bring others to him. Salvation had entered this little town of Samaria.[1]

How moving too is the story of the man who was born blind.[2] This man did not even know who had healed him. He simply bore witness faithfully to what had taken place in him : 'Whether he be a sinner I know not : one thing I know, that whereas I was blind, now I see.' In vain they tried to influence him, to put him on his guard against this unknown man : and all he could say was this : 'Why, herein is the marvel, that ye know not whence he is, and yet he opened mine eyes . . . if this man were not from God, he could do nothing!' And this man, hounded out of the synagogue, met Jesus for the second time. How simple was the act of faith of this man who had been doubly liberated : 'Lord, I believe. And he worshipped him.'

Jesus is not content to bring those who believe in him into the joyful liberty of the children of God : he wants them in their turn to go out and release others, for by the power of the Spirit the word which they have received, and which has set them free, will become an overflowing fountain of strength and light for those who will listen to them.[3]

To believe in him is to pass from darkness to light, from death to life, from bondage to liberty.

[1] John 4.1-30, 39-41.   [2] John 9.   [3] John 7.37-39.

14

THE LIBERTY OF THE MAN CON-
DEMNED TO DEATH

Read Mark: chapters 14 and 15; John: chapters 18 and 19

LET US RE-READ the story of the trial of Jesus as it is
told in the four Gospels. Let us look at this scene: the
arrest, by night, in the garden on the Mount of Olives; the
treachery of Judas; the tranquil 'It is I' of the Lord; the
break-down of the disciples; Peter's denial of his Master; a
mock trial based upon the evidence of false witnesses; the
embarrassment of an official who knows that he is going
to condemn an innocent man; the soldiers who jeer at him,
the crowds who shout . . .

Confronted by all this, the impressive silence of the accused, and in his few words, what calmness and what
authority!

Who is free? and who is enslaved?

Look at Annas and Caiaphas: they are the guardians of
the ecclesiastical order, of the religious tradition, of the con-
cordat with Caesar. For them this rabbi who proclaims
the destruction of the Temple, who attracts great crowds,
is a public danger. They are afraid that he will destroy the
good relations which the authorities in Israel are trying to
maintain with the Roman State! 'It is expedient for you that
one man should die for the people, and that the whole
nation perish not.'[1] This is the main point in the story. The
church authority feels menaced in its prestige, in its power,

[1] John 11.47-53.

in its very existence; it poses as the champion of the Jewish people. The defence of the institution has become more sacred than justice and truth.

Look at Pilate: a Roman official, that is to say, a man who by his training has a certain feeling for equity, for legality, and also a certain knowledge of men. He is swift to detect intrigue; these quarrels among the Jews manifestly do not interest him. He very soon sees that there is no motive for a serious charge. He tries to save Jesus. But the Jews are all very excited. Pilate is afraid of fresh disorder breaking out: Rome does not like riots, and the blame would fall upon him, Pilate. 'Pilate sought to release him: but the Jews cried out saying: "If thou release this man, thou art not Caesar's friend".' This time his mind is made up. The favour of Caesar is worth more than the death of one man. Let us make no fuss! This is what is often called 'for reasons of state'.

Must we speak of Herod? he was the only man about whom Jesus did not hide his disdain,[1] in whose presence he did not utter a word:[2] Herod was the born 'collaborator', he was in the pay of Rome, and was a usurper of the Jewish throne; he was like a jackal who fed on the 'tit-bits' thrown to him by the great ones of this world.

The Pharisees are there too. For a long time past they have been hunting Jesus down with their suspicions and their hatred, and that to the point of joining forces with the Sadducees whom they detested. Jesus challenged their theology, their security as 'right-thinking' men (in their own eyes), men who believe that they are in the correct relation both with God and with men. They are prisoners of their system, of their pride as doctors of the law, of their theology.

And then there is the crowd, that poor crowd which shouts whatever its leaders tell it to shout. Its only policy is to do in Rome as Rome does. It mocks him who has done nothing but acts of love in their midst. 'Save thyself', they

[1] Luke 13.31-32.   [2] Luke 23.8-15.

shouted as they saw him on the Cross. These 'masses' are the plaything of every kind of propaganda.

And the soldiers? they are playing with dice to while away the boring time of waiting while they are on duty; yet it was they who later showed some pity, and offered him a sponge dipped in vinegar.[1]

Peter had denied his Master; he was driven to this only by the ironical remarks of a servant girl. The other disciples had fled—or almost all of them; they were overwhelmed with a terrible feeling of uncertainty. Had they, after all, been deceived? Was Jesus, after all, not what they thought?

Some women are there, faithful, and overwhelmed with sorrow.

This is the human picture which is presented to us. These people were not more wicked than others. They were only cowardly; some feared for their lives if they did not do as the others did; others were defending either their position, or their prestige, or the 'established order'. Their fears, their interests, their prejudices, kept them in chains. But they did not know that they were in bondage. They did not know that *they themselves were prisoners*.

These men simply represent our humanity in its blindness, its egoism, and its pride. It only needs a riot—and some bloodshed—for these passions to be unleashed—when man sinks to the animal level.

And there, facing these people, stands the prisoner: what strength there is in his silence. His eyes look at Peter, and Peter breaks down. His eyes look at the shouting mob and he prays: 'Father, forgive them; for they know not what they do.' Before the Sanhedrin when he is accused, he replies: 'Ye shall see the Son of man sitting at the right hand of power, and coming with the clouds of heaven'—an affirmation, as he is well aware, which will help to condemn him. But the truth must be proclaimed.

To Pilate, who was surprised that this man did not beg

[1] John 19.28-30.

him to be lenient, he spoke very simply: 'Thou wouldest have no power against me, except it were given thee from above.'

Jesus alone knows whence he comes and whither he is going: no one is taking his life away from him; he is giving it, himself, and he knows why.[1] That is his supreme liberty.

Suddenly all the other people look like poor little toys—blind instruments of a destiny which is far beyond them.

And now, behold, at the climax of his torture, he who 'cannot save himself', with sovereign power looses the bonds of the man who is hanging on the cross at his side: 'Verily I say unto thee, Today shalt thou be with me in paradise.'[2] This brigand on his cross is set free.

'It is finished.'

The earthly career of the liberator is over. And already the grain of wheat falling into the ground is bringing forth its first fruits: the conversion of the Roman centurion who was the one who witnessed his agony from beginning to end.[3]

[1] John 10.11, 17-18.   [2] Luke 23.39-43.   [3] Mark 15.39.

PART THREE

THE LIBERTY OF THE CHRISTIAN

15

THE APOSTLES: LIBERATED MEN

THE BOOK OF the Acts of the Apostles shows us, in an amazing way, the liberating power of the Spirit in these men who had been so timid, so cowardly and so apprehensive, only a short time before. Look at Peter. A few weeks earlier the ironical remarks of a servant girl had frightened him so much that he went the length of denying his Master; yet *now* he publicly proclaims his faith before great crowds, in the heart of the Temple, and before the Sanhedrin. The Jewish leaders themselves were astonished by this simple, firm attitude of assurance: 'Now when they beheld the boldness of Peter and John, and had perceived that they were unlearned and ignorant men, they marvelled; and they took knowledge of them that they had been with Jesus. And seeing the man which was healed standing with them, they could say nothing against it.'[1]

What had happened to these men?

The collapse of all their hopes, the darkness of Good Friday, had been followed by the dawn of Easter, and the descent of the Holy Spirit, the revelation of a pardon and a power which made all things new. And the moment that these men had been set free, they turned to the work of helping others to become free too; a great wave of faith and love swept through this new-born community;[2] bonds were broken; people gave their hearts to God, and shared their possessions with their brethren. For to them repentance meant turning their backs on their former life; it

[1] Acts 4.13-14.   [2] Acts 2.37-47.

meant being free, and at God's disposal, for the service of their brethren.

This humble community, meeting in some private house in Jerusalem, did not know that it was about to revolutionize the world. But these Christians could not keep silent. Their joyful liberty had broken down all the walls behind which people would like to keep them; no prison could silence them.

How simple and dignified is the reply of the Apostles to the chief priests who want to impose silence upon them: 'But Peter and John answered and said unto them, Whether it be right in the sight of God to hearken unto you rather than unto God, judge ye; for we cannot but speak the things which we saw and heard.'[1] There is a hierarchy of authority: God is Supreme.

This is the foundation of the liberty of the Christian with regard to the authorities of this world, whether they be ecclesiastical or civil. It is the final court of appeal, and it is the divine one. The calm liberty of the Apostles, a direct reflection of their Master, we find again and again all through the history of the Church in times of trouble and persecution; for instance, in Joan of Arc's statement 'God must be served first'; in Luther's words 'Here I stand! I can do no other'. Our own epoch has seen trials in which the liberty of the Christian believer has more than once disconcerted his judges. Thus in a most impressive way Christ's promise to his disciples has been verified: 'And when they lead you to judgment, and deliver you up, be not anxious beforehand what you shall speak: but whatsoever shall be given you in that hour, that speak ye: for it is not ye that speak, but the Holy Ghost.'[2]

Here we come to the very heart of this authentic liberty, which is a gift of the Holy Spirit.

This 'grace' of the Holy Spirit is blowing like a fresh breeze through the whole story of these early days of the Church, narrated in the Book of Acts. Nothing has yet been

[1] Acts 4.19.   [2] Mark 13.11.

organized. On the other hand, it would be a mistake to idealize the Primitive Church; it was not composed of 'saints' or 'perfect' people; very soon it was to know the pressure of interior tensions.

One of the earliest instances of such tensions occurs in the story of Ananias and Sapphira. No constraint was imposed on the Christians save that of love : they were free to give away their possessions or to keep them. Ananias and Sapphira wanted to give the impression that they were like Barnabas and the others, and that they were ready to 'give all'—which was not true. They were 'putting on an act' of generosity. Why was this duplicity so serious in the eyes of the Apostle? It was because they had 'lied to the Holy Spirit'.[1] They came under the condemnation of Jesus : their true father was not *God*, but the 'Liar', the 'Father of lies', and the fruit of this bondage is death.

There is a second example of such tension in the story of the conversion of Cornelius, a Gentile. The Spirit is free, and he breathes where he will. And behold, here he is, moving in the heart of a Gentile, and a Roman officer at that! The Church was taken by surprise and was much embarrassed. She had not foreseen such a happening. All Peter's conviction was needed to overcome their instinctive opposition to the whole proceeding, and to help them to 'glorify God' for it.[2] Alas! the Church is always so slow to understand the love of God in its infinite height and length, and breadth and depth.

In point of fact, the questions which were raised by the conversion of the Gentiles, were to trouble the Apostolic Church for a good many years. The first Christians were Jews, who were loyally attached to their own laws and customs. They continued to go daily to the Temple, while they gathered together in their private houses to listen to the teaching of the apostles, to pray, and to break bread together.[3]

[1] Acts 5.1-6; cf. John 8.44.   [2] Acts 10 and 11.1-18.
[3] Acts 2.42-46; 3.1; 12.12.

What was going to happen to Gentiles who had been converted? Was it not legitimate to ask from them the same observances, to impose the rite of circumcision upon them? Judaism had many proselytes who were called 'proselytes of the gate' because they could not enter the court of the sanctuary reserved for believers. These were men who believed in the One and Only God, but whom the exigencies of the Jewish law kept, as it were, on the fringe of the community. A Jew did not eat with an uncircumcised person; he was regarded as 'impure', 'unclean'. Should a Jew who had become a Christian fraternize, and even *eat* with Gentiles? who had not been circumcised? It may seem strange after all that we have seen of the liberty of Jesus, of his preaching, that the Church of Jerusalem was so slow to understand that a new age had begun. But that too is very human. In actual fact this Church was divided: on the one side, were extremists, the 'conservatives', who were attached to the letter of the Law; on the other side, there was Peter, open as we have seen to the movement of the Spirit, but conciliatory and rather timid; and there was . . . Paul.

If the conservative party had won the day it would have been 'all up' with the Mission of the Church: Christianity would have remained a Jewish sect.

God had struck one gigantic first blow in the conversion of the Gentile Cornelius. His second blow was the conversion of the fiercest persecutor of the Church: Saul of Tarsus, the apostle to the Gentiles, the apostle of liberty.

Such are the ways of God. Such is the liberty of the Spirit.

Just because Saul was a 100 per cent Pharisee who had put all his trust in the Law, he was able to see what no one else had yet perceived: that is, either, that the Law saves us, and then we do not need Jesus Christ; or, Jesus Christ saves us, and himself becomes our 'law'—the Living One who gives us life. On the road to Damascus, confronted by the Risen Lord, Saul saw the futility of all his

works of the law; he had lost his own righteousness.
Henceforth he lived solely on the grace of Jesus Christ.[1]

The 'I' of the Pharisee Saul of Tarsus with all its works
has been nailed to the Cross of Jesus Christ judged and condemned. That is what enabled the apostle to exclaim 'For
I through the law died unto the law, that I might live unto
God.' 'I have been crucified with Christ; yet I live; and yet
no longer I, but Christ liveth in me.'[2] Henceforth St Paul
had one aim only in life: to know Christ, and the power
of his resurrection, and the fellowship of his sufferings.[3]
What do these words mean?

When we say of someone: 'I know him' that may simply mean 'yes, I know that he exists'. We know his name,
his face, his voice. Or it may mean that we have read about
him and know the story of his life. How many people do
we know? Love alone enables us to enter truly into the
life of another person, to divine his thoughts, to share in
his struggles and his hopes.

When the Bible says that God 'knows' us, it means that
he knows everything, that he reads our most secret
thoughts.[4] When Jesus says that the Father knows him and
that he knows the Father, he means that between himself
and the Father there is a perfect communion of love and
of will. He wills all that the Father wills.[5]

To know Jesus, is first of all to know that we are loved
by him and saved by him. It means believing in his word,
loving him, obeying him. It is a knowledge which takes
up the whole of our being: heart, intellect, and will. To
know Jesus, is to know that he is the Living One, it is to
let him live, and act within us, and to transform us into
his likeness. To know the power of his resurrection, is to
believe in his victory over the demons, and over all the
forces of death.

To know the 'fellowship of his sufferings' means accepting the fact that my egoistic 'self' must be nailed with him

---

[1] Phil. 3.4-10. [2] Gal. 2.19-20. [3] Phil. 3.10.
[4] Ps. 139. [5] Matt. 11.27; cf. John 5.19; 10.14-15.

upon the Cross in order that his life may triumph in us and spring up unto eternal life. It also means entering into the battle against all the forces of evil which are still at work in the world.

This is what gives meaning and direction to the life of the Apostle. Jesus has taken hold of Paul, and Paul is hastening towards Jesus. He is running towards that great day when he will know the Lord, even as he has been known by him, when he will belong to him altogether, free with his freedom, loving with his love. He loves to call himself 'his slave', for Jesus has redeemed him.

But to belong to Jesus Christ does not prevent us from being fully *ourselves*, and not someone else. When we admire a man, sometimes we try to 'copy' him; and copies are always dull. We cannot copy Jesus. We can only open ourselves to his action.

Jesus Christ, when he entered into the lives of the Apostles, bestowed upon them their vocation as persons, each with his or her own particular vocation: Paul remained 'Paul', and John was still 'John'. But all their latent possibilities expanded, in an original and personal way.

This is the liberty of a life which is *given*, like that of the Lord himself; a liberty which will manifest itself like our Lord, in the service of God and the brethren.

It is this liberty which radiates from every page of the Epistles of St Paul, all through all the troubles and trials of a ministry which was most extensive, most heavily burdened, and more full of hindrances and frustrations that one could ever imagine. Wherever Paul went, the power of his message 'troubled the city'.[1]

Persecuted by the Jews, suspected by others, hunted down, beaten, left for dead, he always began again somewhere else; neither prison, nor hunger, nor cold, nor nakedness, could stop him.[2] He did not let himself be dazzled by the wisdom of the Greeks; he did not allow himself to be cast down by the slanders of his enemies. Always and

---

[1] Acts 16.20; 19.23. [2] II Cor. 11.23-27.

everywhere he willed only to confess 'Jesus Christ and him crucified'.[1]

A prisoner, he is free. Dying, he lives. For Jesus Christ is his liberty. Jesus Christ is his life.

16

FIRMLY ROOTED IN LIBERTY

Read Galatians 3.15-4.14 and chapter 5

'FOR FREEDOM DID Christ set us free: stand fast therefore, and be not entangled again in a yoke of bondage.'[2]

The term 'set us free' is an allusion to slavery. From what slavery have the Galatians been set free? Into what kind of servitude is there a danger that they will again fall?

We know very little about the Galatians; they were pagan tribes settled on the high tablelands of Asia Minor, and probably of the same origin as the Celts of ancient Gaul. 'At that time', says Paul, 'not knowing God, ye were in bondage to them which by nature are no gods.'[3] Doubtless they offered sacrifices to appease the anger of their gods; they lived in superstition and fear. And they were given up to the 'desires of their own hearts'. St Paul gives us a picture of paganism which is very dark. For men who are at the mercy of their instincts become the slaves of their passions.[4]

The Apostle Paul arrived among the Galatians. He 'placarded' 'Jesus Christ Crucified' before their eyes;[5] O! what would we not give to know how Paul did this! How he 'placarded' Jesus Christ to these pagans! It is clear, how-

---

[1] I Cor. 1.18—2.5.   [2] Gal. 5.1.   [3] Gal. 4.8.
[4] cf. Rom. 1.18-32.   [5] Gal. 3.1.

ever, that this preaching made a profound, and indeed an overwhelming impression upon them. They realized : 'there is a God who *loves* us! . . . a God who has gone the length of giving his Son to die for us, in order to save us!' The Galatians believed this good news; the Holy Spirit engraved it on their hearts. They were delivered from all their fears; their whole life was changed. They now possessed this joyful liberty which comes with the certainty of the love of God and his forgiveness.

So their gratitude to the missionary who was their spiritual father was extreme! He came amongst them suffering from a painful malady; and he says himself that if they could, they would have 'torn out their eyes' and given them to him.[1]

And then the Apostle had to leave them. Some time later alarming news reached him. Other Christians had visited the Galatians, and must have told them something of this kind : 'Yes! yes! of course Paul is a very good man; but he is not one of the twelve apostles appointed by Jesus; he hasn't told you everything; if you want to be true disciples of Jesus you must accept our Law; you must be circumcised; you must keep the Sabbath and the New Moon and the great festivals . . . It is *we* who are the true believers from Jerusalem, and we are the true Church!'[2]

These poor Galatians were quite new to the faith. All this made them feel quite bewildered. Their old religion laid down certain rites which had to be performed on certain days in the year. Perhaps they had been wrong to give up all that so soon? So they were troubled and disturbed. They lost their happy confidence. They were no longer sure of their salvation . . . they were impressed by the words of these newcomers.

St Paul reacted to the news with a letter which may seem very severe : people have come to disturb his child-

---

[1] Gal. 4.12-15. Perhaps he was actually suffering from eye trouble.
[2] That is why Paul defends (a) his apostolic authority and (b) his doctrine (2.15—4.11).

D

ren, to take from them that joyful liberty which the Gospel
had given them! There is only one Gospel, he tells them,
the good news of Jesus Christ which I proclaimed to you.
If something else, some kind of 'law' could have saved us
then Jesus Christ would have died for nothing.[1]

The Apostle knew from bitter experience that the Law
does not save man, for he had tried that way, and it
had led to his condemnation.[2] Jesus Christ entered into
his life as One who pardons, heals, and makes 'all things
new'.

The Galatians too had known the power of this pardon
which flows from the Cross. They had received the Holy
Spirit. 'Are you going to fall back into the Law?' says Paul.
Then he quoted the example of Abraham who believed the
promises of God and was saved by his faith. The Law
played the part of a 'pedagogue' in the history of the
Chosen People, of a schoolmaster who instructs a child. But
now that Jesus Christ has come does this child want to go
back to the kindergarten?

Salvation consists in this living relation with the Lord
who died and rose again for us: he has done for us what
we could never do. He alone has the power to put to death
the 'old man' within us, and to create the 'new man'. And
this salvation he offers to all; Jews who have been circumcised, Gentiles who are uncircumcised; masters and slaves,
men and women.[3]

In the sight of God, all of us, whether slaves or free in the
sight of men, were victims of the same bondage, the bondage of sin; we are all under the condemnation of the Law,
doomed to death. All, by the grace of Jesus Christ, have
passed from the state of slavery to that of sons and
daughters of God![4]

Then St Paul continues: 'are you going back to "the
weak and beggarly rudiments"?' i.e. to their previous religion with its practices, superstitions and fears?[5]

---

[1] Gal. 1; 2.15-21.   [2] cf. on this point: Rom. 7.
[3] Gal. 3.1-14, 21-29.   [4] Gal. 4.1-7.   [5] Gal. 4.8-11.

It seems to St Paul that here there is nothing for it but to begin all over again. These children whom he has begotten to the world of faith, has he got to go through all the pain of travail a second time?[1]

Now we understand better what the Apostle means when he exclaims: 'For freedom did Christ set us free; stand fast therefore, and be not entangled again in a yoke of bondage.' For where the Galatians had become uncertain involves nothing less than salvation through grace. They had not understood that Jesus Christ alone could save them; that he, and he alone, is their righteousness, their peace, their liberty.

But what does this freedom mean? Does it mean that because Jesus pardons us we are free to sin?

Among St Paul's enemies there were certainly some who caricatured his thought by saying: 'Sin, in order that grace may abound!' 'No indeed', St Paul exclaims, in his Letter to the Romans, for the liberty which Jesus gives us consists precisely in this, that the 'old man', the man of the 'flesh' is condemned, dead, and in his place there is born, by the power of the Holy Spirit, a new man: 'Even so reckon ye also yourselves to be dead unto sin, but alive unto God in Christ Jesus.'[2]

Thus the liberty which Jesus gives us makes us servants of God and of our brethren. 'Through love be servants one to another.' The whole of the Old Law is summed up in the commandment of love. This commandment still holds good; but now it is Jesus Christ who lives it in us, who animates us with his love through the Holy Spirit.[3] In him this Law, which used to crush us, has become what St James calls 'the law of liberty', and the believer finds his happiness in the very act of obedience itself.

St Paul then describes for us the 'fruit of the Spirit'. This consists of love, joy and peace; patience, kindness, generosity, fidelity, courtesy, and self-control. Thus faith does not dispense us from 'works'. It produces them just as in-

[1] Gal. 4.19-20.   [2] cf. Rom. 6.1-11.   [3] Gal. 5.13-26.

evitably as a good tree bears good fruit.[1] But it is Jesus
Christ who produces this fruit within us; so there is no
cause for pride or boasting.

We have seen what the liberty of Jesus Christ means;
we have seen that Satan has no power over him; we have
seen that his will was wholly one with that of the Father,
that his heart beat in union with the Father's heart; we
have seen him giving his life freely for his brethren.

It is this liberty which he wants to communicate to us;
it is this liberty which he wants to live within us.

'Hereby know we love, because he laid down his life for
us: and we ought to lay down our lives for the brethren.'[2]

We know very well that we do not suddenly pass from
the bondage of the old Adam which is selfish, proud, self-
centred, to that glorious liberty which is that of Christ.

We shall only know the fulness of his love and of his
freedom in the world to come. But we count on him; we
look up to him; in him, by faith, we have the earnest of this
future liberty. And if we allow his Spirit to act within us
he does transform us 'into his likeness'. We discover more
and more, even we, that 'where the Spirit of the Lord is,
there is liberty'.[3]

What does this mean, in practice—for my daily life?

It means that I commit the past with its sins, its failures
or successes to the Lord; that I am no longer the slave of
my past; that I do not look back.

This means that I can live fully in the present moment;
taste and enjoy all human joys as a gift which God gives
to me, and endure all the sufferings and conflicts, because
my Lord bears them with me.

This means that I can look forward to 'tomorrow' without anxiety and without panic, for the Lord knows this
unknown future; he has prepared it; and he will go through
it with me.

Thus he communicates to me his own liberty, with re-

[1] Gal. 5.22; cf. Matt. 7.16-20.   [2] I John 3.16.   [3] II Cor. 3.

gard to people, things, and circumstances. In him is given
back to me the world with all the possibilities, all the
riches, which the Creator has placed within it.

The liberty of the Christian allows him to enjoy without
scruple, and indeed with fresh intensity, all that the world
offers that is beautiful and good.

But it also means that we are to use the things of this
world as though they were not[1]—that is to say, we can do
without them when they are denied to us; for our real
treasure is elsewhere.

That is the joyful liberty which the Lord wills to give
even in this life to his own.

17

NECESSARY DISCIPLINE

Read 1 Cor. 9.24-27; Phil. 3.12-16; Eph. 6.10-20

DOES THIS CHRISTIAN liberty of which we have just
been speaking dispense us henceforth from all discipline?
If we were to believe this we would fall into a dangerous
confusion of thought, against which St Paul puts us on our
guard. He, the Apostle of liberty, does not hide from us
that he imposes a severe discipline upon himself; and that
for two reasons: in order not to fall into temptation; and
in order to be more wholly at God's disposal, to be able
to 'run' in the service of Christ.

What difference is there between 'the law' which the
Apostle rejects, and the 'discipline' which he accepts?

What St Paul rejects is the law as a means of salvation,
or the effort to establish our own righteousness. The Phari-

---

[1] I Cor. 7.31.

see believes that he is right with God because he observes all his legal obligations. A Catholic may feel sure that he is right with God because he goes regularly to Mass; a Protestant may think he is a 'good Protestant' because he is a 'decent man', who has never stolen from anyone or killed anybody . . . But all the time this Pharisee, this Catholic, this Protestant, may have no love in his heart. Such people are wholly self-righteous. They know nothing of the grace of Jesus Christ; they do not know that at the Last Day, whatever they have done, their only hope is in 'grace' alone.

One who is 'constrained' by the love of Christ[1] will give him the obedience of love. He will strive with all his might to give him the first place in his own life, and to make him known to others. This discipline, freely accepted, will never be a 'merit' for him. It will simply be the expression of his faith, of a life *given*.

Thus the Christian will be all the more faithful to his humble daily duties because this great love of God has entered into his life. For true love is measured by fidelity in little things.[2] All his life now belongs to the Lord : 'To do little things as though they were great things,' says Pascal, 'because the Lord does them in us; and great things as though they were little things, because of his Omnipotence.' So our daily work, even if it may seem very humble and not very interesting, now takes on a new meaning : it is the actual concrete situation for my obedience; it is *here* that the Lord asks me to serve him. And because he is with me in my work, because he has taken charge of my whole life, and thus also of my work, because this work, however imperfect it may be, is now placed under the sign of his grace and his pardon, I can accomplish it in freedom and in joy.

St Paul knew the discipline of his calling; he earned his living as a tent-maker; it was his pride to be able to preach the Gospel for nothing. He regarded the obligation of work

---

[1] II Cor. 5.14.   [2] Luke 16.10.

as a Christian duty: 'If any will not work, neither let him eat.'[1]

The Apostle uses two favourite metaphors to describe the Christian life: that of the soldier, and that of the athlete. Whether we are speaking of the life of a soldier or of a sportsman, both imply discipline.

'No soldier on service entangleth himself in the affairs of this life; that he may please him who has enrolled him as a soldier. And if also a man contend in the games he is not crowned, except he have contended lawfully.'[2]

The Christian belongs to the army of Jesus Christ.

The Kingdom of God, the interest of the Kingdom, comes first. All this must come before the trivial affairs of this life.[3] The life of a Christian is that of a soldier on active service. In order to resist all the forces which assault him from within and without he needs nothing less than the 'whole armour of God'.[4] There are defensive weapons: the righteousness, the truth of Jesus Christ envelop us like a protective breastplate. There are offensive weapons: the sword of the Word and prayer.

The sword of the Word is called here the 'sword of the Spirit'; it is by the Holy Spirit that the word of Scripture becomes 'living and active, and sharper than any two-edged sword, and piercing even to the dividing of soul and spirit, of both joints and marrow, and quick to discern the thoughts and intents of the heart'.[5]

This living word, which speaks to us throughout the Bible, who has been 'made flesh' in Jesus Christ, judges us, calls us, consoles us, and directs us. To listen to him ever anew, to be nourished by the Word, that is the first discipline of the Christian. It will be his daily protection, both defensive and offensive, the power by which he will overcome the world and will purify his own heart. For him this will be a perpetual school of liberty: 'If ye abide in my word, then are ye truly my disciples, and

---

[1] II Thess. 3.6-10.   [2] II Tim. 2.3-5.   [3] Luke 12.22-34.
[4] Eph. 6.10-18; cf. I Peter 5.8-9.   [5] Heb. 4.12.

ye shall know the truth, and the truth shall make you free.[1]

The second weapon of the Christian will be prayer; the prayer of the Church, to which each of us will contribute his or her own prayer; we are then supported by the rest, and we support them in their turn; here also the supreme Intercessor is Jesus Christ himself, who stands in our name before the throne of God. He prays for us; we pray in him and through him. We watch with him, he watches over us and in us. Prayer is like the discipline of the sentinel, who stands at his post, waiting in faith for the great Day of the Lord to dawn.[2]

The second favourite metaphor of St Paul, as we have said, is that of the athlete, who runs a race in the stadium, or of the gladiator. He must, I imagine, have often been to the Games in the stadium at Tarsus, when he was young, to watch the Games so much enjoyed by the Greeks.

The runner has his eyes fixed upon the goal: the crown which he hopes to win. While he is running, that alone exists. Thus St Paul, 'apprehended by Jesus Christ', looks only at him, and is running towards him, in order to carry off the prize of the immortal crown. And he invites the Church also to run towards this goal, to have but one thought in common, the Lord who comes, for whom she waits, whom she serves, of whom she wants to be worthy . . .[3]

St Paul tells us that he treats his body harshly and keeps it under.[4] This may surprise us: was it not enough for him that he had to drag about a body all over the place which was already in poor condition and often sick into the bargain, and must he inflict on it all the privations which were inseparable from a ministry like his?[5] Is Paul an 'ascetic', who thinks that bodily privations have a special merit? Certainly not. But he knew that it was necessary to discipline his body and his senses. He wants to make his body an obedient and supple instrument of the Spirit. The life

[1] John 8.31.
[2] Isa. 62.6; Mark 13.32-37; 14.38-39; Luke 17.31-32; Rom. 8.26-34.
[3] Phil. 3.12-16.   [4] I Cor. 9.24-27.
[5] cf. II Cor. 11.23-28; 12.7-10.

of the body is not a matter of indifference : the body is the 'temple of the Holy Ghost'; transformed by the Spirit it will participate in the final resurrection. That is why, he says, 'all things are lawful for me, but I will not be brought under the power of any'.[1] This is a salutary reminder for us who live in a time like ours when there is so much temptation to live an easy life, in which the life of the senses claims to be all important.

In addition to the discipline of the body there is the discipline of the mind; we are not to let our minds wander 'all over the place'; we are not to run in a haphazard way, nor to 'beat the air'. The Christian is a person who knows where he is going. He neither speaks nor acts at random. God has given direction to his life, once for all. He will discipline his thoughts, his words, his actions; he will be careful about his use of time, in order that everything may contribute to the final aim.

And it is this self-mastery which will make him a free man—free for God, and free for the service of his brethren.

Above all, he will allow himself to be disciplined by God himself. God alone knows what we need; he moulds us into true liberty by the trials and chastisements, the joys and consolations, which he sends us. For what son does not the father chastise?[2] God is the great surgeon who opens up, one by one, the wounds which are most hidden—but he does this in order to cleanse them, in order to heal them. He shows us where we are still 'enslaved', although we were unaware of it—in order to set us free completely.

Thus the work of liberation goes on all through life. 'Work out your own salvation with fear and trembling', says St Paul again, 'for it is God which worketh in you both to will and to work for his good pleasure'. You are under grace; God in Jesus Christ has done everything for you: *that is why: Work!*[3]

[1] I Cor. 6.12-20.   [2] Heb. 12.4-11; cf. II Cor. 12.5-10.
                        [3] Phil. 2.12.

18

THE ORDER OF CHARITY

Read 1 Cor. 3; 8; 12-14

THERE IS ONE temptation which dogs the footsteps of
the Christian who has experienced Christian freedom : that
of affirming this liberty in and out of season, and of despis-
ing the brother who is less free than himself. Because he
has reached a certain stage of inward liberty, a certain independence of judgment—because he believes that he has
reached spiritual maturity, he thinks he has the right to
judge others. He thinks that he alone possesses the Holy
Spirit! . . .

If our freedom does not function in the heart of the
Church, in the fellowship of the brethren, in the 'yielding-
ness' of mutual love, it runs the danger of degenerating
into individualism, or party-spirit; it may crumble into
pride or anarchy. The 'self' re-appears in a new form, more
odious than before. In self-complacency or indifference
such a Christian may trample upon 'the brother for whom
Christ died'. When this happens, the meaning of the Cross
has been forgotten.

This is the danger which seems to have threatened the
Church at Corinth. And the way in which Paul deals with
it, in this particular instance, will help us to see more
clearly the limits which love—concern for the life of the
community—will set to our liberty. Because there may be
something we want to do which, in itself, is quite legitimate, yet which, for our brother's sake, we ought to forego.

At Corinth there were people who felt very strong, and

thought they were very wise and advanced in the faith. The scruples of other people may have seemed ridiculous to them. One subject which caused much discussion was that of meat which had been offered to idols. Was it allowable to eat such meat? The 'strong' people said: 'Of course! This is not important because the idols don't exist!' But the 'weak' people were uneasy and troubled in their consciences.[1]

They decided to consult the Apostle Paul. Of course the 'strong' people thought that he would take their part and say that they were right! Had he not said repeatedly that in Jesus Christ we have been set free from the Law? But St Paul's verdict was quite different from that which they had expected: 'it is agreed', he said to them, 'that you and I see clearly on the question of meat offered to idols, but knowledge puffs up, whereas love builds up. Our knowledge and our "enlightenment" is useless if we have no love. It is true, of course, that the idols don't exist! but if some people are troubled by the fact that this meat has been offered on the altar of an idol, then be careful, and don't tempt them to eat it!'

'Take heed lest by any means this liberty of yours may become a stumbling-block to the weak. For if a man see thee, which hast knowledge, sitting at meat in an idol's temple, will not his conscience, if he is weak, be emboldened to eat things sacrificed to idols? For through thy knowledge he that is weak perisheth, the brother for whose sake Christ died. And thus, sinning against the brethren, and wounding their conscience when it is weak, ye sin against Christ.'[2]

It is the thought of the *brother* which dominates the argument. Note that when Paul had to do with the Jewish-Christians of Jerusalem who were the 'strong', and wanted

---

[1] I Cor. 8; 10.23-33; cf. Rom. 14. The flesh of animals sacrificed in heathen temples was afterwards eaten at home or sold in the market. Those who refused to eat such meat were reduced to eating 'nothing but vegetables'.
[2] I Cor. 8.

to impose their views upon the Gentiles he had resisted. But here it was a different matter; St Paul's point is this: that we ought to be willing to renounce something which we feel perfectly free to do, so far as we are concerned, in order that some 'weaker brother' should not be led astray.

This question of meat sacrificed to idols seems very remote to us today. But the principle laid down by St Paul, the concern that we ought 'not to cause a brother to offend', is still contemporary. In a heathen setting, even today, participation in a certain family ceremony or a particular rite or dance may present dangers for a new convert. He may feel himself caught up by demoniac forces from which he has hardly been freed,[1] while for someone else such action would have no significance. He who is set free from his fears will take care not to be the cause of a fall for one who is not yet entirely liberated from his former fears.

Some Churches think it right to lay down rules for their members about drink, smoking, dancing etc. while others claim that they have Christian liberty, and leave such decisions to the choice of the individual. The risk of imposing such rules is to generate a new kind of Pharisaism: the people who accept it think that they are good Christians —better than others—because they do not do this or that; they judge the brethren from the height of their own virtue! If this were correct then our virtues would save us and not the Cross of Christ! That is what St Paul calls 'coming again under the yoke of the Law!' But what is required is a discipline which is freely accepted for the sake of others, or because we know our own weakness; such abstentions can only command respect.

A pleasure which is innocent for one person may be full of dangerous suggestions for another. I do not see any reason why I should not drink a little wine, but if my example becomes a temptation to someone who is tempted to drink far too much, then it is my duty to abstain. My

[1] I Cor. 10.19-22.

behaviour is conditioned by that of the brethren around me. I ought to help them to find in Jesus Christ a liberty which will enable them to use the things of this world without becoming enslaved to them, and without scruple. At the same time I ought to put myself in their place, take their situation into account; and not let them be tempted to fall into temptation. I think that this is what St Paul means when he says: 'for though I was free from all, I brought myself under bondage to all, that I might gain the more' . . . 'that I may by all means save some'.

'To the weak I became weak, that I might gain the weak: I am become all things to all men, that I may by all means save some.'[1] Jesus Christ alone can give us this liberty which enables us to be 'all things to all men', while, at the same time, we remain faithful to him. This is the liberty of a love which seeks human beings where they are, and takes into account the setting in which they have lived and existed all their lives. Such love is patient; it waits for God's hour to strike: for love 'beareth all things, believeth all things, hopeth all things, endureth all things'.

Paul compares the Church to a building, or to a body, in which all the parts are closely articulated. The interest of the whole should always control that of the parts. For if 'one member suffereth, all the members suffer with it; . . .' 'The eye cannot say to the hand . . . I have no need of thee . . .' This interdependence of all the members of the body is the limit set by God to the liberty of each one. Here too the story of the Corinthian Church is a good example for us today.

These Corinthians thought they were 'strong' and 'free'. But in point of fact, says the apostle, 'in reality you are at the kindergarten stage of the Christian life . . . you are still only "babes in Christ" because you are full of "jealousy and strife"'.[2] Their religious assemblies showed to how great an extent each person thought only of himself. The fraternal meals were a sorry sight: each person gobbled down

[1] I Cor. 9.19-23.   [2] I Cor. 3.1-8.

his own food without thinking of the others at all.[1] The Holy Communion service was profaned. In their meetings for prayer, they all wanted to speak at once, and those who had the gift of 'speaking with tongues' thought they were superior to the rest.[2] St Paul observes that they only edify themselves because no one understands them, and he adds: 'I had rather speak five words with my understanding, that I might instruct others also, than ten thousand words in a tongue.' The central idea of the whole of this fourteenth chapter of 1 Corinthians is that above all we must always look for what will build up *the Church*. Then we shall subordinate our personal freedom, our personal edification, to the common good.

St Paul here lays down a principle which is essential for all community living: that of liberty combined with order, order with liberty. He summons the Christians to submit themselves to one another in the fear of Christ.[3]

But when we mention 'order', it raises the question of 'authority'. From the Christian point of view, what is the place of authority?

19

AUTHORITY AND LIBERTY

Read Luke 22.25-27; Phil. 2.1-16; 1 Peter 2.13-25; Eph. 5.21-6; 6

MANY PEOPLE NOWADAYS think that liberty and authority are two mutually exclusive terms. 'To be free', in their view, means to be free from any obligation to account for our actions to any other person; it means being

[1] I Cor. 11.17-22.   [2] I Cor. 14.   [3] Eph. 5.21.

one's own master. The child rebels against his parent, the workman against his employer, those who are governed against those who govern. Behind these forms of revolt, very often there lies a false conception of authority on the part of those who govern, as well as a false conception of liberty in the mind of those who have to obey.

Hence it is important to enquire into the Biblical idea of liberty, and also that of authority. What change of attitude is the Lordship of Jesus Christ going to make in the mutual relations between those who rule and those who obey?

In the preceding pages we have tried to define Christian freedom. We have seen that communion with Jesus Christ delivers us from our past, and enables us to be at the disposal of God and man, for their service. Thus the new self which has been given to us, does out of love that which we previously did from constraint. My service, whatever it may be, will be *free*, if I have *freely accepted it*, that is, if, in serving men, I am worshipping and serving God. Thus the Apostle Peter, exhorting the members of the Church to submit to human authorities, is able to say: 'as free, and not using your freedom for a cloke of wickedness, but as bondservants of God. Honour all men. Love the brotherhood. Fear God. Honour the King'.[1] This means that Christians are to respect the civil authorities and be subject to them, 'because of the Lord'. Note the shade of meaning: we are to '*fear*' no one but God. It is his displeasure alone which we must take care not to incur.

The apostles base their exhortations to obedience on two essential motives: first, because all authority comes from God (we shall be coming back to this point a little later on). Then, secondly, because Jesus Christ came amongst us as 'one that serveth'. He endured injustice; the Christian will think it an honour to suffer something for God, because then he will be treading in the footsteps of his Lord . . . 'Christ also suffered for you, leaving you an example that ye should follow his steps: who did no sin, neither was

[1] I Peter 2.16-17.

guile found in his mouth: who, when he was reviled, reviled not again; when he suffered, threatened not; but committed himself to him that judgeth righteously . . .'[1]

Thus the liberty of the Christian will be manifested in a
submission to which he consents, in the gentleness and
serenity with which he freely accepts this trial. It is by this
voluntary submission that the slave will be a witness of
God to his master, that the wife may win her husband.[2]

Thus if the obedience lived in Jesus Christ become a witness to the grace which is at work within us, where does
authority come in?

Here there are two distinct questions which must be
faced.

(1) What is the basis of human authority?

(2) Does the authority of the believer gain, in Christ, a
new meaning?

Let us first of all examine the Biblical conception of
authority. The Bible recognizes only one absolute sovereign
authority: that of God. He is the Lord of heaven and earth.
We have seen the apostles take their stand against the
established authorities in the name of this sovereign authority. 'Whether it be right in the sight of God to hearken
unto you rather than unto God, judge ye: for we cannot
but speak the things which we saw and heard.' This answer
of the Apostle Peter to the Sanhedrin is an appeal from the
Jewish ecclesiastical authority—whose legitimate authority
he does not question—to God himself, the final supreme
authority. Here we touch the limit of human authority:
the point where it contradicts the commandments of God
and where Christian liberty asserts its rights; but this can
only be done in the name of a higher obedience.

Within these limits, obedience to human institutions is
correct. 'Let every soul be in subjection to the higher
powers: for there is no power but of God; and the powers
that be are ordained of God. Therefore he that resisteth the
power withstandeth the ordinance of God: and they that

[1] I Peter 2.18-25.   [2] I Peter 3.1-6; 8-17.

withstand shall receive to themselves judgment . . .' The rôle of the magistrate, says St Paul, is to encourage good and to punish evil, for 'he is a minister of God to thee for good'.[1] The word 'minister' means 'servant';[2] the allusion is to service to the city (or the municipal government) parallel to that of the priest in the religious sphere. It is rather striking that St Paul applies this expression to the Roman authority, which was a heathen government. Did not Jesus Christ, too, say to Pilate: 'Thou wouldest have no power against me, except it were given thee from above?'[3]

The Lord said that at the moment when he was being unjustly condemned. He has no illusions about Pilate; but since Pilate is there, in this position, it is because it has pleased God that this should be so. Jesus does not question the right of Pilate to put him to death; it is to God that one day Pilate will have to give an account of his actions, whether they were just or unjust.

Doubtless St Paul too had no illusions about Roman justice; but without the Roman order there would be chaos; thus the Roman order, however limited it might be, was not only an expression of the will, but of the grace of God. It ought to be respected.

The Old Testament already recognized a hierarchy of functions, each function involving particular responsibilities: the authority of the father in the family, of the chief of the tribe, of the king for the nation. Likewise, in their own order, there was the authority of the magistrate to execute justice, of the priest to watch over the order of worship, of the prophet as the bearer of the word of God. Each sphere of authority had its rights and its duties. In the sight of God to fail to execute justice was as serious a sin as its abuse. Every one will have to render an account to God of the way in which he has exercised the mandate

[1] Rom. 13.1-4.
[2] 'Deacon': used both of an official of the Church, and of the holder of a religious office outside Christianity. (Translator.)
[3] John 19.11.

with which he was entrusted for the good of the community. For each of these authorities renders a 'service' for the common good, and all this 'service' should be rendered to the community as a whole.

The New Testament does not change any of the social and political structures which then existed; they are 'of this world' and will pass away with it. The revolution wrought by the coming of Jesus Christ is more profound, and of another order: for he came to found a new community governed by other laws. Jesus himself noted the contrast between the two orders—that of this world, and that of his own.

'And he said unto them, The kings of the Gentiles have lordship over them; and they that have authority over them are called Benefactors. But ye shall not be so: but he that is greater among you let him become as the younger; and he that is chief, as he that doth serve. For whether is greater, he that sitteth at meat, or he that serveth? is not he that sitteth at meat? But I am in the midst of you as he that serveth.'[1]

In this new society, which is the Church, there are still those who govern and those who serve. But the Lord who controls all authority in earth and in heaven, is the One who has come 'in the form of a servant', and was obedient even unto death.[2] Thus one who wields authority in the Church in the name of Jesus Christ has no glory of his own: he too is under obedience. The real significance of this service lies in the fact that it is exercised in love and in humility. Here liberty consists in being stripped of all self-interest, of all dictatorial love of power, as well as of all false timidity.

St Paul illustrates this change of attitude in two particular instances: in the marriage relationship, and in the relation between master and slave.

On the plane of salvation the Apostle affirms that 'there can be neither Jew nor Greek, there can be neither bond nor

---

[1] Luke 22.25-27.   [2] Phil. 2.1-15.

free, there can be no male and female : for ye are all one (man) in Christ Jesus'.[1] All are objects of the same grace, all are heirs of the same promises. All are intended to enjoy the status of the 'glorious liberty of the children of God'.[2] We ought to realize what a revolution has been effected by Christianity in giving to woman, to the slave, their full human dignity, their status as children of God. We have seen that the attitude of Jesus with regard to women astonished the men of his day; it is due to his example that woman today owes that respect which gives her her place within the Church alongside of man, a place which she never had within Judaism, nor in pagan antiquity.

But from this new state of affairs St Paul does not draw the conclusions which they seem to involve for us, the people of the twentieth century. He did not proclaim the emancipation of women nor the abolition of slavery. What then did he do?

He simply shows that for those who are in Jesus Christ all human relationships have entered a new dimension. The presence of Jesus Christ in those who belong to him transforms both the idea of authority and that of obedience, because both are transcended by love.

This Christian liberty gives to husband and wife in Christian marriage a stability which is due to the fact that it establishes them in a submission which is both mutual and freely accepted : each belongs to the other, but each too has his and her vocation as man and woman.[3]

Paul claims that the husband ought to love his wife *as Jesus Christ loved the Church*. How has he loved it? in taking it under his care, in giving his life for it; in coming to his own 'as one who serves'. What is proposed to the husband is nothing less than an imitation of Jesus Christ; that is, he will love his wife to the extent of being ready to give his life for her; he will take care of her; he will be faithful to her, he will watch over her, he will give her the freedom

[1] Gal. 3.26-29.   [2] Rom. 8.21.
[3] Eph. 5.21-33; cf. Col. 3.18-19; I Cor. 7.3-5.

Jesus Christ has given to the Church. We can see how much
this means in a world where until quite recently woman
was still regarded as an inferior being.

On the other hand, woman, by the gift of herself, will
be a symbol of the Church which is submissive to her Lord.
She will find her joy in this service, which is freely accepted.

In such a relationship, both the spirit of domination and
that of servility are excluded. Each respects in the other
the mission with which God has entrusted him; they grow
together in this liberty and this mutual confidence, which
the certitude of forgiveness and of the grace of God alone
can give us—and give us back again and again when we
have lost it.

So far as the slave is concerned, we have already seen that
the Apostle regards his very condition as an opportunity for
witness; for he now will do willingly what he previously
did only under constraint. He will do it 'for the Lord'. But
what about the master? He will be just and fair, knowing
that he too 'has a master in heaven', and that in the sight
of God there is no respect of persons.[1]

Writing to Philemon on the subject of Onesimus, the run-
away slave whom he is sending back to his master, St Paul
bases the relation between master and slave upon an entirely new foundation. Legally he admits the rights of the
master; he does not ask him to set his slave free. But in one
sense he asks a great deal more, for he asks Philemon to
receive Onesimus as a 'brother beloved', as he would wel-
come the Apostle himself.[2]

In Christ, in the Church, there can only be *brothers* and
sisters; all distinctions of race, sex, and class disappear at
the Table of the Lord; all alike are only 'sinners saved by
grace'. But in the Church there is a diversity of functions
according to the gift which God has given to each one; each
function should be recognized and honoured. St Paul calls
himself voluntarily the 'slave of Jesus Christ'; but it is pre-

[1] Col. 3.20—4.1; cf. I Cor. 7.20-21; Eph. 6.5-9.
[2] Philemon, verses 8-21.

cisely in his quality as apostle, as the messenger of Christ, not speaking in his own name, that he expects to be obeyed. The liberty of the faithful will be expressed in their mutual submission, in the humility with which they recognize the gifts of others, and obey their own leaders.[1]

Thus the Church gives the example of *an order in liberty*, in which each, in his own function, sees himself as the servant of the rest, and in which all have only one Master Jesus Christ, who willingly made himself 'in the form of a servant', and because of this was exalted to glory and royalty.

The Church, in being this new community, is a 'sign' to the world of the coming Kingdom of God.

The apostolic Church did not try to reform the city of the ancient world. But the spiritual revolution which was being wrought within it necessarily had to work as a leaven in the world, when the time was ripe for it. All the liberties that the West has won—slowly over the course of centuries —have sprung from this fundamental respect for man as a human being, as God's creation, called to fulness of life in freedom.

We still have to consider the connexion between this Christian liberty, which the New Testament proclaims, and the freedom of every kind which modern man claims as his right.

[1] Rom. 12.3-8; Phil. 1.1; 2.1-12; Heb. 13.17; Eph. 5.21.

PART FOUR

20

THE LIBERTY OF THE CHRISTIAN AND HUMAN FREEDOM

THE STORY OF our salvation, as the Bible tells it, is simply the record of a long journey towards freedom.

God has given to man, among all his creatures, the possibility of saying NO to him; he could have obliged us to obey him; but then we would only have been marionettes whose strings he would have pulled, or slaves whom he would have ruled as a despot. But God wanted to have *sons* who would respond freely to his love.

In contrast to the first man who claimed his own liberty, and immediately became a self-willed murderer, God has set the Second Man, Jesus Christ, the Son, who gives himself freely to his Father and to his brethren. Thus the real question for each of us is this: which kind of liberty will we choose? of 'Adam'? or of Jesus Christ? that is: whether I shall be a person who clamours arrogantly for my 'rights', or someone who *gives* himself, willingly, to the service of God and man.

The Old Testament shows us God training his people for liberty; this People was still a child; God put them under the Law. St Paul compares this law to a 'pedagogue' (a schoolmaster) who educates the child, prepares him for the day when he will attain his majority, when he will have to take his own responsibilities upon himself. With the coming of Jesus Christ the New Age begins; to be in the school of Jesus Christ, is to live by faith, and no longer under the Law. Christ alone, as we have seen, has the power to make us free men, who give themselves freely. The Church is this new community, governed by Jesus Christ, in which liberty and authority are not two opposing principles, but two necessary principles which complement each other; all authority and all liberty are ordained by God. For one who has to rule, what matters always is to educate those under his charge in the meaning of their responsibility towards God and men; the aim of all education will be to train men for freedom.

Parents ought to know how to make their children obey them. A dangerous sentimentality leads some modern educationalists to believe that we ought always to explain to a child *why* he ought to obey. It is a poor preparation for life, in which we often have to obey without understanding the reason why! But if the authority of the parents reflects the authority of God, then it will be both firm and wise; it will create a relationship of mutual confidence; and the child will learn to trust his parents even when he does not understand their intentions. Gradually, as he grows older, an appeal will be made to his sense of responsibility; that is to say, his parents will have to take the risks of liberty, i.e. he will have to bear the consequences of his own decisions.

This is how God treats his children. It is the hard apprenticeship of freedom! There is a risk that a child who is kept too long under authority, will never become a man, that he will suffer from 'infantility' all his life.

If we take this vocation to liberty—to which God calls every man—seriously, it will have consequences in the social and political sphere. The miracle of the Gospel, as we have seen, is that a slave can be a free man inwardly, in spite of the fact that he is a slave. Similarly, a prisoner, if he is set free by Jesus Christ, can become a free man, in spite of prison bars; just as the inhabitants of an occupied country can remain free in spite of the occupation : Jesus himself lived under Roman occupation!

But the miracle which permits a man to know the grace

of Jesus Christ in spite of the conditions which life imposes upon him, does not justify the existence of these conditions.

The Bible makes explicit statements about the conditions under which a man who works for his living ought to be treated: these affect his wages, his leisure, and his liberty.

It tells us that the cry of the oppressed reaches God. It wills that each person should cultivate fully all the faculties which God has given him, in order that he may share them with others in the service of God and the brethren. This also implies that whole human communities ought to be able to develop along the line of their own culture, with their own language, and in the light of their own particular genius.

That is why, in the name of justice, in the name of the dignity of man, Christians, during the nineteenth century, fought for the abolition of slavery, for the abolition of certain kinds of work which exhausted or degraded people, and for universal education.

That is why in the twentieth century Christians are fighting for the rights of subject peoples to order their own affairs, for the attainment of political liberty.

Liberty of the Worker

From the Christian point of view, in what does the freedom of the worker consist?

It does not exclude a diversity of functions: in all organized labour, both specialist and manual workers are required; there is a need, at every grade, for men who can organize the work, and have the responsibility of giving orders. Moreover the dignity of the worker means that he should not be treated as a 'thing' or a 'hand' but as a *man*, that his work should be recognized and respected, that he should have the possibility of choosing his particular job and have his gifts used; that he may rejoice in the good things which the Creator has placed at the disposal of men —to found, feed and house a family, to have sufficient rest, to educate oneself, and to remain in contact with the land, and with nature.

These external conditions are of course not enough to make a man free. But they do enable him to bear his responsibilities as a man, to be fully himself to use the gift which he has received from God. We ought to fight to make it possible that everyone should have this kind of liberty.

We who are Christians will remember at the same time that the secret of liberty lies in a life given to God and to man.

What does this mean in the sphere of work? We regard it as service; we will do it 'unto the Lord'; we will look at our daily work as the sphere of obedience. However harsh or monotonous it may be, it will have meaning and value if we accept it willingly for the love of God and our brethren. Do we not know that the Lord is in charge of our whole life, which includes our work? Henceforth he is with us in our work; he bears its joys and its difficulties with us. The only work which we cannot offer to him is one which involves destruction or deceit, for God can only use something *living*.

The liberty of the citizen and the politician

How does the liberty of the Christian express itself in the sphere of citizenship? We live in a very complicated world, in which it becomes more and more difficult for the ordinary citizen to form a personal opinion on the questions which affect the future of his country.

Politics is a terrible game in which the forces of money, intrigue, personal and collective forms of egotism often interfere with care for the common good, with justice and law. The politician ought to take account of the economic, social, and international factors over which he has no control; his choice is limited; he is obliged to take into account at every moment what is actually 'possible'. In his decisions, of all men he is often the least free.

The first duty of the Christian—of every Christian—will be to pray for men who wield power;[1] to ask that they may

---

[1] I Tim. 2.1-4.

have all the powers of discernment, wisdom, and courage, which they need, in order that they may act in the most conscientious manner possible, and be able to resist the pressure which is exerted upon them from many directions.

But the Christian cannot confine himself to this; he cannot contract out of his responsibilities because they are difficult. He cannot get rid of his political obligations in order to 'keep his own hands clean'. For he is part of all that concerns his country as a citizen. He has his own responsibility for this in the sight of God.

The liberty which Jesus Christ gives us permits us both to love this world—this world for which he gave his life— and also to look at it with realism, without illusions.

Our political activity also must be without illusions. We know that nothing is pure, and all our actions will have to be forgiven. There is no absolute save God.

Thus we shall refuse to become immersed in Utopian dreams which do not take into account the actual facts, the concrete realities which the politician must face. We shall know that there are some kinds of compromise which are inevitable. We shall accept the painful tension which always exists between our faith and the realities of this world.

This means that we cannot speak of 'Christian politics'. No politics can be 'Christian' in the true sense of the word. That is why we believe that it is dangerous to form 'Christian parties'. There are only Christians who *go into politics*, where they try to act to the best of their knowledge, and in harmony with their conscience. Now and again they will form groups, when it seems wise to do so, in order to do some special study, or to take some common action. But they will be careful not to label such political action 'Christian'.

Although politics concerns the sphere in which everything is relative so that it is always burdened with compromise, there are limits beyond which the Christian cannot go. If he is asked to break promises which have already been made, if in the interests of political 'efficiency' he is asked to take measures which violate the principles of justice, or the fundamental liberties of the nation, which are recognized by the country's laws, he ought to say *no*. For the end does not justify all kinds of means. In so far as he is a Christian he will keep his freedom of judgment, even should certain refusals ruin his career. He will recognize that the State has the right, and indeed the duty, of maintaining order, if necessary, by force; but he will not accept the statement that might is stronger than right.

We live in an age when propaganda wields a terrible power. It ends in controlling public opinion, which makes men its playthings. It is on this plane that the liberty of the Christian ought to be affirmed. He will then know how to resist the passionate reactions which occur in a country in a time of crisis. He will try to obtain reliable information, and to see things clearly. This is not easy!—he will not blindly follow the opinion of his own particular circle, or of a particular newspaper, or of the radio.

We live at a time when material interests tend to become man's main preoccupation. People think in terms of 'output', 'efficiency' and 'production'; on the plane of economics all this is legitimate. But this may reach a point at which man is only regarded as an instrument of production, a cog in the wheels of the great industrial or administrative machine.

The Christian who has been trained in the school of Jesus Christ knows that 'man does not live by bread alone'. He knows that the human person has an infinite value in the sight of God. He knows that in a civilization in which material interest is the main motive, where man loses his liberty and his dignity as a man, ends in destroying itself. He knows that a country which loses the sense of the meaning of justice and law is drifting into chaos. The whole Bible contains this warning.[1]

[1] See in particular what is here said about the message of the Prophets.

It is because he knows all this that, as a Christian, he has a special responsibility for the fate of his own country.

But Christians, people will say, are often a very small minority! It is not the number that matters, but the force of their conviction and the firmness of their attitude; the liberty of the Christian will often manifest itself in the courage with which a man will go against the main current, and will dare to brave public opinion. He will know what he has to say; he will not ask whether he will meet with success or failure, but only what is right and just. This presupposes of course that he knows what he is talking about, and is objective and impartial in his judgment.

There are other people, as well as Christians, who are courageous men, who put truth above party politics, and who defend the law when it is in danger of being violated. The Christian will support them, in whatever party they may be, when a just cause is at stake.

At a time when so many nations are moving towards political independence (whether partial or total), the Christians in these countries will remember that the right to vote does not make a man free. The Churches of these countries have a great part to play in such a situation : will they know how to train men of character? of whom their country has need? men whose moral integrity is above suspicion? men who draw from Jesus Christ the secret of true liberty, men who, in their trade union, in their town or parish, in the councils of their country, will be the builders of a human community based on mutual respect, upon justice and upon law?

It is on such men that the future of a nation depends.

The liberties which the Church ought to defend

We believe that there are certain fundamental liberties which the Church ought to defend, whether she speaks through the mouth of her official organs, or through the mouth of her members.

First of all, the liberty to preach the Gospel

1. This is the liberty which the Church should never allow to be taken away from her, even though this should expose her to the dangers of martyrdom. She has experienced this in the terrible persecutions which have occurred in the course of her history. She knows this still today. It is quite possible that she will have to experience still worse ones yet! Totalitarian states—whether they are Fascist, Communist or sectarian—know that the Gospel contains a leaven of liberty. The Christian who has been fed and nourished by the Gospel cannot be led away by propaganda like a toy or a thing. He is a dangerous force of resistance in a State which wants to dominate not only the body but also the consciences of men!

In some circumstances the State will engage in an open conflict. More often it will try to limit the action of Christians by a compromise. It will allow them to preach an individual salvation, to speak of 'the next world', but it will tell them not to meddle with this one, here and now! The State will try to draw youth away from the Church, in order to train them according to its own doctrines. It will forbid the Church to take any social action.

The Church must claim for herself the right to preach the *whole* Gospel to *all* men. She cannot allow her apostolate to be limited; she cannot admit, for instance, that she should be forbidden to evangelize non-Christians, and that Christians are to shut themselves up within their own 'ghetto'. She cannot admit that the State should intervene in her life and impose an ideology upon her which is foreign to her belief: for instance, by insisting on her obeying racial laws, or by trying to use her as a channel for political propaganda. The Church will serve the State best by maintaining her own liberty; by showing in her own life what a community of free and responsible persons, all engaged in the same service, and always ready to put the interest of the whole above that of their own interest, is like.

2. And because the Church demands that her own liberty should be respected, because Jesus Christ calls us to the liberty of the children of God, she will also know how to respect the freedom of others. If need be she will champion them. In the history of the Church there have been dark hours when the Church wanted to impose truth by force, by fire and sword. Today we know that nothing is more contrary to the spirit of the Gospel. We ought never to use the arm of the State to force our convictions upon others. We shall remember that Jesus Christ, in order to convert men used no other power than that of the Cross, no other witness than that of faith, sealed upon men's hearts by the Holy Spirit.

And this same Spirit will give to Christians, when that becomes necessary, the courage to obey God rather than men.

3. The first liberty, we have said, that the Church should claim is that of proclaiming the Gospel, the Gospel as a whole.

But this Gospel also insists that it should be the *sentinel* who watches to see that the justice of God is respected in all human relationships. This is the second liberty which must not be taken from her.

She will see to it that respect for the law is encouraged when these laws have been broken. She will set her face against all laws which are contrary to what the Bible has revealed to be the will of God for his children; that is to say, to everything which establishes discrimination between men according to their social standing, or the colour of their skin; to all that tends to destroy the family of mankind.

It is the duty of the Church to warn those who exercise power when they betray their mandate. For they themselves too will have to recognize that they must render an account of their behaviour before the Almighty God—to this God whom perhaps they do not even know. The Church henceforth must care for them as well as for those who are her own members. It is her 'prophetic' mission to be the sentinel of God.

4. But the most important witness which the Church can render to the State will always be that of her own life. What matters is that she should show, by her whole existence, what is the true authority, liberty, and fraternity. She must herself be free from the spirit of competition and domination, from all venality, from all prejudices about class, race, or party. At a time when political passions are a terrible cause of division among men, the Church must never allow these passions to divide her within herself: her members must be able to listen to each other and to treat each other's opinions with respect: after all, have we not the same Lord?

Only thus will she be the witness to this glorious liberty of the children of God, for which the whole creation is waiting with ardent desire.[1] We know very well that this liberty will never be perfect save in the Kingdom of God. We wait for it with faith and hope. But every Christian, every parish, ought to be a *Sign* of this coming Kingdom. For 'where the spirit of the Lord is, there is liberty'.[2]

[1] Rom. 8.19-22.   [2] II Cor. 3.17.